Nicole Wilde

# *Hit by a Flying Wolf*

## True Tales of Rescue, Rehabilitation and Real Life with Dogs and Wolves

Phantom
Publishing

Hit by a Flying Wolf
True Tales of Rescue, Rehabilitation and
Real Life with Dogs and Wolves by Nicole Wilde

Copyright © 2014 by Nicole Wilde

Published by:
Phantom Publishing
P.O. Box 2814
Santa Clarita, CA 91386
www.nicolewilde.com

First Edition

Library of Congress Control Number: 2013921558

ISBN 978-0-9817227-4-0

*For all the dogs and wolves
I have known and loved.*

Other books by Nicole Wilde:

*Living with Wolfdogs*

*Wolfdogs A-Z: Behavior, Training & More*

*So You Want to be a Dog Trainer*

*It's Not the Dogs, It's the People! A Dog Trainer's Guide to Training Humans*

*One on One: A Dog Trainer's Guide to Private Lessons*

*Help for Your Fearful Dog*

*Getting a Grip on Aggression Cases*

*Energy Healing for Dogs*

*Don't Leave Me! Step-by-Step Help for Your Dog's Separation Anxiety*

# Acknowledgements

This is the most personal book I've written, and I'd like to thank the people who supported me throughout the strange and wonderful experiences I've written about.

To my mother, Lisa Terry, thanks for being a great role model, not only as a strong, vital woman, but through your loving, compassionate approach to living with and training dogs. No doubt a love of dogs is in my blood.

Valerie Pollard, you are a great friend and will always be close to my heart. I so appreciate all of your support during the early difficulties with Bodhi.

Tia Torres, we've been through a lot together. No one will ever know all the heartaches (or muscle aches!), or the joy of those wolf rescue days. I've shared just a bit of it here. Twenty-five years later, we're still close friends, and I'm so proud of all the good work you're doing.

Margaret (Margo) Rudoy, thank you for being so good with Mojo and so kind when he was going through therapy. It meant a lot to all of us.

Sheryl Mistretta, I will always appreciate your assistance at the shelter where we adopted Sierra. I'm glad we're Facebook friends so you can continue to see through photos how happy and loved she is.

Adrienne Hovey, thanks for your editing skills and for being so much fun to work with. Having a twisted sense of humor is a prerequisite for editing my work, and you definitely qualify. All hail the Semi-Colon Queen!

Michelle Silmon, you are a soul sister and one of my favorite people. You not only helped with my wolves, but you and Bruce helped so many. You will always be a shining light in this world and in my heart.

C.C., thank you for being so loving and patient through all the crazy dog and wolf years. You're not only a great husband, but such a cool, amazing, and supportive human being. I'm incredibly blessed to have shared the last quarter century with you. You're still my favorite person in the world.

# Table of Contents

Introduction                                                    1

## Part I: The Dogs

1   SoCal and Soko                                              9
2   Of Earthquakes and Rock Stars                              15
3   Into the Desert                                            27
4   The Miniature Christmas Wolf                               31
5   Double Crazy Legs                                          37
6   Don't Leave Me                                             43
7   Sheep Herding—Baaah!                                       49
8   Bazooka                                                    53
9   Deadly Weapon or Enlightened Being?                        59
10  Day Ten                                                    65
11  The Honeymoon's Over                                       69
12  The Peanut Butter Couch Skirmish, Part Deux                75
13  Got Any Pizza or Beer?                                     79
14  Thanksgiving Stuffing                                      83
15  The Cuddle Offensive                                       87
16  Mush!                                                      91
17  The Queen and the Cover Boy                                95

## Part II: The Wolves

18  Two Little Reds and the Big, Mostly Good Wolves            103
19  Wolf Sitting, Pit Bulls and Unusual Humans                 109
20  House for Sale: Two Bedrooms, Two Baths, Three Wolves      115
21  Who's Afraid of the Big Black Brat?                        119
22  Heyoka Visits the Vet                                      123
23  Wolves on the Loose!                                       127
24  Hit by a Flying Wolf                                       131
25  Apocalypse Now                                             135
26  Scorpions, Tarantulas, and Rattlesnakes—Oh, My!           143
27  Living with Wolves                                         151

# Introduction

Phantom was one of the biggest wolves I've ever known. He weighed 140 pounds, and the giant-sized Varikennel added another forty pounds. It must have been the adrenaline rush that allowed C.C. and me to get the crate out of the enclosure and into the road, all while keeping an eye on the fire that was now eating its way much too quickly through the brush. Already at the bottom of the hill, it was racing toward us. At the top of the hill, another set of flames blazed a trail toward the house. There was nothing we could do. C.C. ran up the driveway and got his car. I opened the hatchback of my Jeep Cherokee, and when he returned, we loaded the crate into it. Or, I should say, we tried to load the crate into it. The crate was one I'd borrowed from Tia months before, and somehow I'd assumed that, like the others, it would fit. I cursed myself for being so stupid. How could I not have tried it? Phantom couldn't fit into a smaller crate, and now we were out of time.

"*Nicole*," C.C. said in a stern tone I'd never heard before, "we have to go." He began to walk quickly away from the Jeep, toward his car.

The crate was sitting in the middle of the dirt road, and the fire was coming. "I can't just leave Phantom here!" I cried. Surely there was a way to bring him with us…

But wait. I'm getting ahead of myself. Let me explain how I ended up trying to rescue a wolf from a fire, and for that matter, how I began living and working with dogs and wolves in the first place.

~ * ~ * ~ * ~ * ~ * ~ * ~ * ~ * ~ * ~ * ~ *

As a child, when asked by adults, "What do you want to be when you grow up?" I lacked an appropriate response. Other little girls would say, "A teacher," "A nurse," or even, "A wife and mother." But none of those

1

things appealed to me. What I was interested in—and by "interested in" I mean *crazy* about—was dogs.

The only serious career path I knew of that involved working with animals was that of veterinarian. Unfortunately, my lack of interest in the medical sciences, paired with my distaste for the curriculum requisite of cutting up dead animals, put me out of the running. I place blame for the latter squarely on the slumped shoulders of my high school lab partner who, in a stoned-out haze, had ripped the eggs out of our shared frog with maniacal glee. It didn't help that the heart was still beating after we'd removed it. With veterinary school off the table, I didn't know what sort of future could involve working with dogs. Still, I still longed for one. Although my dreams would not be realized for quite some time, dogs were a constant presence throughout my formative years and provided a warm, furry soundtrack to my life.

Our first dog had begun life with the proper Scottish name "McTavish." My parents, for reasons unknown to my brother Bobby and me, decided his name must be changed. And so, in democratic fashion, we kids were allowed to suggest new monikers. We were so excited! My seven-year-old ideas ran toward darkly descriptive names like "Midnight" and "Onyx." I don't remember Bobby's suggestions, but he was only four at the time and I believe one of his choices had to do with a type of cheese. Suffice it to say the names he came up with weren't anything you'd want to shout across a crowded park. In the end, my father chose one of his own suggestions: *Happy.* I hated the name, but Happy it was.

Happy was, as Scottie pups can be, rambunctious and nippy. He would chase Bobby and me around our small Brooklyn apartment and, if we weren't fast enough, leave tooth marks on our heels and ankles. I quickly developed a strategy of racing to my bedroom, jumping on the bed, and plastering myself against the wall just out of reach of Happy's snappy jaws. Looking back, it seems odd that my mother never called a dog trainer. Then again, it was a different time and trainers weren't on the public radar like they are now. Besides, nippiness aside, Mom always seemed to have a way with dogs. Without ever having read a single book about training, she'd been able to teach Happy to behave well, and to perform a catalog of tricks including Shake and Roll Over. Mom was a natural. Fascinated, I watched what she did, and absorbed my first lessons in dog training.

My mother was also very athletic. Not only had she been an acrobat in her native Norway, performing across Europe in places like the Moulin Rouge in Paris, but here in the States, she was an excellent tennis player and an accomplished bowler. She bowled in a league, and she was very, very good. Our apartment sported a style that could best be described as Silver and Gold Trophy motif. The wall-to-wall bookcases were crammed full of statues sporting proud, winged figurines and plaques that read *1st place—League* or *Individual High Score*. There were smaller, candy-dish style awards strewn across every coffee table, end table, and other available surface as well. Mom finally began to refuse the trophies, having run out of places to put them.

One afternoon when Bobby was five and I was eight, my mother took us along to the bowling alley. The 20-minute walk from our apartment wound through a safe, middle-class neighborhood—safe, that is, except for one desolate stretch that ran under an elevated set of train tracks. In the center of this no-man's-land sat a junkyard filled with cars in various states of disrepair. As many times as we'd passed the metal wasteland, I'd never seen a person inside. I was, however, acutely aware of the large black and tan German Shepherd who patrolled restlessly back and forth along the chain link fence, barking out stern warnings at anyone who dared trespass anywhere near his kingdom. Our collective pace always quickened as we passed.

As we approached the path that led past the junkyard, I didn't see the dog pacing along his usual route. Where was he? Moments later, the answer became horrifyingly apparent. He had escaped. There he was, the beast who had achieved legendary monster status in our juvenile minds, standing not fifty feet away, with no fence between us. He stood still, his head lowered, staring…and then ran straight toward us! Hackles raised, barking furiously, the dog flew at us. Mom pushed Bobby and me firmly behind her as she took a step forward. Facing the dog squarely, she thrust her palm forward in the international signal for "Halt!" The dog, startled, paused mid-stride. She then commanded in a stern, authoritative voice, "Sit!" The dog's rear hit the ground immediately. Mom walked calmly away with us in tow, our hearts pounding wildly. I glanced back. The dog, still seated, wore a most quizzical expression as he watched us leave. What my mother did that day left a lasting impression. Who knows, maybe dog training is in my blood.

When I was twelve, I returned one day from playing outside to find Happy gone. My parents had given him away because of a new no pets rule in the building. We hadn't had a chance to say goodbye; I suppose my parents were trying to save us the grief. Still, Bobby and I were heartbroken. But as children do, we became involved in other things and were able to move on. When I entered high school at thirteen (yes, thirteen…but that's another story), we got another dog. Skippy—you *know* I didn't pick that name, either—was a smallish Schipperke-Lab mix. We'd visited the local humane society, where my parents had quickly spotted her. Just five months old, the black, long-haired puppy was standing her ground in the corner of a crowded pen. A group of dogs surrounded her, barking and snapping, and she was giving it right back to them. My parents liked her spirit.

Despite her early bullying experiences, Skippy grew into a wonderful, well-adjusted dog who loved people and other dogs. I delighted in lying on the floor with her after school, stroking her long, silky black fur and telling her about my day. I had fun teaching her obedience skills and tricks. Skippy was a fast learner and an enthusiastic student. She'd prance about in excitement, eager to spin, give her paw, and roll over. I was so proud of my brilliant pupil.

Skippy was a constant companion to Bobby and me throughout our adolescence. Bobby eventually moved to Long Island, and I attended Brooklyn College. Because I'd been in an accelerated high school program, I began college just after my sixteenth birthday. My declared double major was English and psychology, but what I really majored in was driving motorcycles and dating guys with long hair and black leather jackets. Imagine my parents' delight. After graduating at nineteen, I took up the electric bass guitar and started playing in rock bands, once again thrilling my parents to no end. But I also had to earn a living, and so, a string of office jobs ensued. Whether my hours were spent in a stark grey cubicle or a fancy office, my goal was always to get my work done, keep my head down, and fit in until I could figure out how to get a job working with dogs.

Regardless of where I worked, on the side, I trained dogs who belonged to friends and neighbors. I eventually got a few paying clients. Still, it wasn't enough to support me. And so I persevered in the corporate world, wearing the proper attire (I still say pantyhose are from the devil), dutifully oohed and aahed over baby photos, and discussed television shows that seemed inane but were apparently all-important to my fellow employees. That I had dog photos lining my cubicle walls instead of baby pictures seemed odd to most. Then again, I'm sure I seemed strange to them anyway, with my rock and roll hair and laid back attitude. For me, the days were endless. I was stuck in Stepford. Years later, I was lucky enough to land a job in the music industry, where a more relaxed atmosphere prevailed.

All in all, my life was not bad. I was fortunate to have a rent-controlled apartment, a job at a hip record company in Manhattan, a boyfriend who also happened to be a nice guy, and a few close friends. But I also had a persistent, nagging feeling that I was meant to be somewhere else. And I knew exactly where: California. True, I hated the freezing Brooklyn winters and the noisy, crowded subways, but it was more than that. There was a very real, constant nudging at my psyche to get on a plane and head for the West Coast. It was like being homesick for a place I'd never been.

~ * ~ * ~ * ~ * ~ * ~ * ~ * ~ * ~ * ~ * ~ * ~ *

Little did I know all that California would hold. My life took some amazing twists and turns, and led me to places I never would have imagined. Over the years, I volunteered for city animal shelters and private rescue groups, and served as volunteer coordinator for a Los Angeles city shelter. I eventually became a dog trainer, canine behavior specialist and author, and traveled around the world lecturing on dog behavior. I was privileged to share my life with an amazing man, some wonderful dogs, and even wolves. But I'm getting ahead of myself again.

What follows are stories of working and living with dogs and wolves, from my vantage point as a rescuer, trainer, and dog mom. Some experiences are funny, some are poignant, and some are downright strange. But they're all absolutely true. For ease of reading, I have kept the dog stories and the wolf stories separate, even though both species were living here with us at the same time.

I hope these offerings entertain you, lift you up, and maybe even make you feel better about life with your own dogs. My years with dogs and wolves have been funny, challenging, joyous, and heartbreaking. They've also been some of the best times of my life. As the Grateful Dead say, "What a long, strange trip it's been."

# PART I

# The Dogs

# So Cal and Soko

I was twenty-eight when I finally arrived in California. I didn't know a soul, but a music industry co-worker had suggested I look up a woman she knew there. The woman owned and lived in a two-story bungalow in Los Angeles. After spending an afternoon chatting and hanging out with her I ended up renting the upper level. The second floor was small, but it had a panel of floor-to-ceiling windows that looked out over the Hollywood Hills. At night, the landscape twinkled with stars even brighter than the ones living in the nearby homes. During the days, the shared garden provided a lush sanctuary where I could relax. To this city girl, it seemed like heaven.

A friend had come to stay with me for the first few weeks. As there was only one bedroom, she slept in an alcove off the living room. One night after I'd gotten into bed, I looked out the bedroom door to see my friend standing at the windows, her back toward me. She was wearing a long white nightshirt. In the dim light, I could just make out the back of her head. She slowly shifted her weight from foot to foot as she gazed wistfully across the hills.

"Cheryl?" I called tentatively. "Are you okay?" I figured she was missing her boyfriend back home.

"I'm fine. Why?" The sleepy voice came from the alcove—*not* from the figure I could still clearly see at the window.

"Hang on a sec," I said calmly, and got out of bed. I walked toward the figure, keeping my eyes on it all the while. But when I got a few feet away, it vanished. I felt badly for whoever it was—or had been. After all, a sad person is a sad person, whether they happen to be breathing or not.

The ghost didn't bother me, but the woman downstairs did. She turned out to be a manipulative, emotional drama queen. Well, that was a fine welcome to California! It was also the coldest January on record. The upper floor had no insulation, and the woman decided that I didn't deserve to borrow any blankets. To add to my misery, the car I'd purchased turned out to be a lemon that spent more time in the shop than out. Cheryl returned to New York after a few weeks, and I was on my own. Suffice it to say those first few months in Los Angeles were very difficult.

I eventually got a ghost-free apartment, a car that ran, a job at a recording studio, and a gig playing bass guitar in a local rock band. I made the classic mistake of dating a bandmate, and the relationship lasted ten months. A few weeks after we'd broken up, one of the girls who never seemed to be in short supply around the guys' communal apartment felt sorry for me, and dragged me out to a club on the Sunset Strip called the Coconut Teaszer. I met my future husband that night. C.C. was tall and thin, with long, dark hair that fell in graceful waves almost to his waist. He looked like a rock star, but thought like a poet. He was intelligent, gentle, and fun to be with, and it wasn't long before we fell in love and moved in together.

Hollywood was fun in a something-happening-all-the-time kind of way, but we eventually tired of the constant chaos. Seeking calm and quiet, and a place where we could have dogs, we rented a guesthouse in Woodland Hills, a picturesque suburb at the edge of the San Fernando Valley. The sky blue, split-level cottage had spacious rooms and vaulted ceilings, and was set on a small cement lot in back of the bigger home. A grassy strip ran down the side of the main house. It continued alongside ours, affording us our own unenclosed bit of yard. The entire property was fenced on the back and sides with chain link, but there was no barrier between the main house and the street. Our landlord, Candy, lived in the main house with her soft-spoken, teenage son Mitch, an all-around nice kid and dog lover.

Candy and Mitch had three dogs. Simba, an old Aussie who could barely walk and had to be picked up in the mornings as he lay on the cold concrete driveway. Toke, a young German Shepherd, was as sweet as could be; she was brown, tan, and friendly all over. Peace, her male companion, was a large, intimidating-looking three-year-old black German Shepherd who gave me flashbacks to the Beast on the Way to the Bowling Alley.

Soon after we'd moved in, Mitch led us over to the garage to meet Peace. As he opened the door, a large black blur barked and lunged, scaring the hell out of us. Mitch was able to calm the dog down, but I wondered how we would co-exist. Fortunately, over time, Peace began to live up to his name—that is, unless we returned home after dark. Once night fell, all bets were off. We'd park on the street and tiptoe past the main house. Ten feet to go, then five…but Peace would inevitably hear us and begin to bark ferociously as we passed. Luckily for us, he was tied out at night on a long rope that put us just out of reach.

Over time we not only befriended Peace, but we also discovered his secret: he was an addict. If there were twelve-step meetings for dogs, he would have been standing on his hind legs at a bone-shaped podium, declaring, "My name is Peace and I am a fetch-aholic!" No doubt the Malamutes would have woo-woo'd a warm, "Welcome, Peace!" The other Shepherds would have nodded knowingly. The Border Collies, of course, would simply have stared.

Peace's drug of choice was a tennis ball, but he'd make do with anything he could get his jaws around. Sticks were plentiful on the property, and he'd often approach C.C. and me, tail wagging in excitement. He would deposit a stick at our feet and look up with a glint in his eyes as if to say, "C'mon, it'll be fun!" He had us trained in no time. When he couldn't find something solid for us to throw, he'd pick up stray scraps of litter, or even leaves, and beg for a game. Ever try throwing a leaf? It's not easy. The compulsive aspect of Peace's behavior was a bit sad, but we enjoyed playing with him and indulged him whenever we could.

~ * ~ * ~ * ~ * ~ * ~ * ~ * ~ * ~ * ~ * ~ *

Finally, C.C. and I decided it was time to get our first dog. I had my heart set on a long-coated German Shepherd puppy. I searched shelters and rescues, but had no luck. Finally, we located a breeder. The woman informed us that the long coat was considered a fault in breeding lines, but she did happen to have one of those "mistakes" in the litter. One person's fault is another's find, and we soon brought home a beautiful black and tan German Shepherd puppy. We named her Soko. My favorite drink at the time was Southern Comfort and Coke—SoCo and Coke for short—and I thought the name was clever. (And here I'd laughed at Happy.) C.C. rounded up some fencing materials and turned our grassy strip into an enclosed yard, where we delighted in playing with our energetic bundle of fur. We took Soko everywhere we could, socializing her in unfamiliar environments with a variety of people. I taught her obedience, manners, and tricks, took her to training classes, and introduced her to other dogs.

Soko was a quick learner with a scary-smart intellect. She'd do something once, and *get* it. Like Peace, she was completely ball-obsessed. If no one was available to throw a tennis ball, she would amuse herself by standing at the top of our staircase, dropping the ball, and then racing down the stairs to retrieve it. She'd often place a ball near my feet as I sat eating dinner, and then go into her routine: she would look at me, and then look at the ball. Me. The ball. Back and forth, back and forth. The thought bubble over her head clearly read, *Toss it already!* She was a Border Collie in a German Shepherd's body. I have no doubt she could have held that stare, unflinching, for hours. When I would finally tire of being stared at, I would turn to her and say calmly but firmly, "Not now." Since I'd taught her that meant no further attention would be forthcoming, she would pick up the ball, trot over to her dog bed, and lie down with a heavy, drama queen sigh.

Like me, C.C. had always had an affinity for dogs. He'd grown up with a much beloved Collie named Sparky. But he had lived in the Appalachian mountains of North Carolina, where the culture was not exactly pet-centric. Dogs were used for hunting more often than they were house pets. The very idea of a dog living indoors was alien to him. When we got Soko, I informed him that she'd be living in the house; whether he would be as well was up to him. I was only half joking.

Soko was a happy, well-adjusted dog that first year. But after a traumatic experience (more on that soon), she began to display major anxiety issues. Most people don't realize that dogs can have a genetic predisposition to sound phobias, where the telltale behavior doesn't surface until something triggers it. And Soko's most troublesome issues were definitely noise phobias. Certain sounds—specifically, sharp, high-pitched ones—would send her into a near-panic. Watching television became a tense experience for us all, as sooner or later a program or commercial would include a high-pitched beeping that would send Soko rocketing from the room.

Although there were a variety of sounds that could set Soko off, beeping was the one I most wanted to desensitize her to, particularly since she'd developed a fear of the microwave oven. The issue could be traced back to the beeping of C.C.'s pager. She had been afraid of the sound, and being a smart dog, had quickly generalized the fear to other things that created a similar tone. She knew that the microwave beeped, and that the door opening and closing preceded the scary sound. Then she deduced that food being taken out of the freezer meant the microwave door would soon open, which predicted the scary sound. She quickly back chained the sequence to the freezer door opening. Finally, she'd run any time I even approached the kitchen. Although fleeing the kitchen was a perfectly understandable response if you'd eaten my cooking, in her case, it was completely unnecessary.

To tackle the problem, I positioned C.C. at the microwave with instructions to open and close the door gently on my cue. We would work up to the beeping sound. I stood with Soko at the far end of the house, a handful of hot dogs at the ready. As planned, C.C. gently opened and closed the door. With each repetition, I fed Soko a piece of hot dog. Things were going along nicely until something—perhaps a wayward burst of testosterone—caused C.C. to slam the door shut. The result? For a week, Soko was afraid of hot dogs! Fortunately, after that, we were able to get back on track with the desensitization program.

Although she was sweet and highly intelligent, it would be safe to say that Soko was no Lassie. Once, during a winter storm, the ramp outside our back door iced over. I stepped outside, slipped, and went down in a most ungraceful heap. My ankle hurt like hell, and I suspected it might be broken. I began to cry from the pain. Did Soko, with her genius doggy intellect, run to the phone and dial 911? Did she bark until help came? Nope. She disappeared, and soon came trotting back…with a ball in her mouth. She dropped it where I sat, and proceeded to look from me to the ball. Back and forth, back and forth…*Gonna throw it or what?* Nope, not Lassie by a long shot.

Although C.C. had always treated Soko kindly, her constant fears and anxieties made it difficult for him to feel truly close to her. And as much as I loved her and was sympathetic about her fearfulness, I had to admit that I would have loved to have had an easier dog. But looking back, I can appreciate how much Soko taught me about working with fear issues. Her challenges would end up indirectly helping other dogs in the future.

Of course, we only wanted what was best for Soko, and one thing we knew she would enjoy was a canine companion. By the time she was eleven months old, she'd had plenty of training and behavior work, and it seemed like the right time. The dog who would become Soko's lifelong companion was Mojo, a German Shepherd-Malamute-Rottweiler-wolf mix who was larger than life.

# Of Earthquakes and Rock Stars

We all love our dogs, whether they happen to be cute or ugly, well behaved or holy terrors. But every now and then a dog comes along who is truly special, a dog who touches the heart so deeply and connects to the spirit so strongly that it's clear no other dog who comes after will ever affect us in the same way. Some call this their *heart dog* or *soul dog*. My soul dog was Mojo.

Tall and thin, with long, dark hair, he moved with a self-assured swagger. Where other dogs had admirers who offered compliments like, "She's so adorable!" or, "He certainly is a handsome boy," Mojo had what I can only call *fans*. At 120 pounds, he was taller and longer than most dogs. Although some people were afraid to approach him, many wanted to run their hands through his shiny black fur. I couldn't walk him down the street without someone stopping us to exclaim, "Wow! What kind of dog is that?" Mojo was a mix of Alaskan Malamute, German Shepherd, and Rottweiler, with a smidge of wolf thrown in. He had a little bit of everything, and a whole lot of charisma. He was a rock star. A friend once confided, "Mojo is the reason I have dogs." She'd been a cat person all her life but had, like so many others, fallen under Mojo's spell. The dog she adopted, Salem, looked like a smaller version of our boy.

Mojo had come to us through an unusual series of events that began at 4:30 a.m. on January 17, 1994. Although it would later be dubbed the Northridge Earthquake, the epicenter of the horrifying incident was not actually in Northridge, California as originally thought, but some ten miles south, in Reseda. We didn't need a seismologist to pinpoint the exact location. It was our living room. One minute I was sleeping peacefully, and the next I was sitting bolt upright, certain that a freight train was about to smash into the house. An insanely loud roar filled the air. The walls trembled. The bed shook violently. In panicked confusion I ducked and swerved, trying to dodge the hardcover books that flew from a high shelf at my head. I screamed into the pitch-black room at the top of my lungs, but I couldn't hear myself. In the living room, where C.C. had been sleeping due to a bad cold, things weren't any better. A 100-pound oak cabinet filled with record albums crashed to the ground inches from his head.

Stumbling around in the darkness, terrified and disoriented, we somehow found each other in the hallway. We grasped hands and did our best to step over and around the shards of broken glass and rubble, carefully inching our way toward the front door. I reached for the knob but the door was locked. Of course it was; we always locked it. But at the moment neither of us was thinking clearly. We groped around in the dark, trying to find the keys. Suddenly, I smelled gas. Just then I heard Soko barking. She'd apparently fled through the dog door to the back yard at the first sign of trouble. I couldn't blame her. Envisioning the house exploding from a gas leak, we frantically redoubled our search efforts. Finally, we found the keys and made it outside. All in all, the violent shaking had lasted 20 seconds. It had seemed like 20 minutes.

Buildings had collapsed. Trees had smashed into cars. People were injured. We were all in shock. The rest of the world was just hearing the news, but it was still far from over for us. Aftershocks—tremblers that are normally weaker than the original earthquake—can happen minutes, hours, or even days after the initial jolt. Each time an aftershock began, I thought another quake was coming. Adrenaline surged, and my body went into fight or flight mode. I couldn't help it. Others in our area were similarly affected, judging from the number of neighbors who had pitched tents and camped out on their front lawns, too frightened to go back indoors. Soko was perhaps the most traumatized of all. Each time the trembling began, her body would tremble along with it. We took turns hugging her tightly, as it seemed to calm her somewhat.

Not a single thing in our house had been left standing, save a computer hutch. We cleaned up as best we could and stayed inside. I expected things to settle down, but those aftershocks just kept coming, one after another. It was exhausting mentally, physically, and emotionally. After the fifth or sixth aftershock, it all caught up with me. I was in a state of complete and utter torment. I turned to C.C. and said, "I don't know if I can live in California anymore." We'd always discussed New Mexico as a potential place to live, and so, with the walls still shaking, we decided to at least get out of town for a few days. I had a friend who lived outside the quake zone, and Soko loved to play with her dogs. I knew Soko would be far calmer there than where she was now. And so, we left Soko in good hands and headed for Albuquerque.

Friends had advised us that the New Mexico climate was much like southern California's. Hah! Not once during the entire time we'd lived in L.A. had it snowed in January. And yet, there we were, shivering under a cold, white blanket of frost. We'd intended to drive up to Santa Fe, but there was so much snow that the highway was closed. On the bright side, at least the ground wasn't moving. We sat in our hotel room eating cereal and bananas and reading the local newspapers. I noticed an ad in the Classifieds section. "Wolf Hybrids," it began. "Sweet, wonderful family dogs." While I took the description with a grain of salt, it had me intrigued. We'd been wanting to find a companion for Soko, and here we were, all snowed in and nowhere to go. And, the breeder happened to live very close to our hotel. We looked at each other and shrugged. I made the call.

I don't know what I was expecting a breeder of wolfdogs to look like— perhaps a beautiful, exotic Native American or a gruff Road Warrior type—but Stacy and her husband looked like typical suburbanites. The slim brunette and her stout, muscular husband were welcoming as they led us through a wooden gate into their back yard. A chain link pen sat in the middle of the dirt lot, but the wolfdogs were out and about. Deva, the mother, was a beautiful white Malamute-wolf mix. She was soft in every way, from her long, silky fur to the way she sidled up to us for petting. Her long, slender snout tickled my face as she planted soft, wet kisses on my cheeks.

Then there was Thor, the father. A German Shepherd-Rottweiler mix, he stood a few feet away, glaring. Although he didn't lunge or otherwise threaten us, he might as well have been wearing an "Unwelcome" sign. It was clear that we were trespassers. Stacy explained that while Thor wasn't dangerous, he'd never been particularly friendly toward people. It speaks to how long ago this was and the state of my post-earthquake brain that I didn't take that red flag, wave it for all it was worth, and high-tail it out of there.

There were nine pups in all. At eight weeks of age, the adorable bundles of black, tan, and white fur were wrestling, romping, and having fun as only puppies can. As we approached, some kept right on playing, while others, full of curiosity, walked toward us. Two of the pups hung back and regarded us warily. Having left my anti-cuteness shield at home, I found myself at the mercy of big, brown eyes and joyfully wriggling bodies. I sat on the ground playing with the puppies, oohing and aahing, sinking into a blissful stupor. Blame it on oxytocin, that blasted cuddle hormone. It facilitates nest building in birds and acceptance of offspring in sheep, and turns adult humans into simpering messes around puppies. Damned if I wasn't flooded with the stuff. Cuddlemania ensued.

Visions of crates and health certificates danced in my head. Still, we hadn't planned on bringing a puppy home in the midst of the earthquake upheaval. We told Stacy we were unsure. In an attempt to help us come to a decision, she told us about Dave, an auto mechanic who had one of Deva and Thor's offspring from a previous litter. She was sure Dave would be happy to let us visit his nearby shop and meet the now year-and-a-half old Zeus, who he took to work with him daily. We jumped at the chance to get a preview of what the puppies might grow up to be like.

After fifteen minutes of carefully navigating a maze of grey, slushy roads, we arrived at Dave's shop. I walked through the front door with C.C. a step behind. No sooner had I placed a foot over the threshold than a mass of black fur and fangs flew at me. Zeus stood on his hind legs, placed his paws on my shoulders, and snarled into my face. I was dimly aware of approaching footsteps. Standing perfectly still with my eyes cast downward, I thought, *I sure hope this guy has good control of his dog.* "Zeus, *off!*" Dave yelled. With a final glare that said, *We'll finish this later,* the bear of a dog dismounted and reluctantly retreated. Dave apologized and explained that he usually put Zeus away when customers arrived, but he hadn't had the chance. What was it with Thor and Zeus and these terrible attitudes? I made a mental note to never name a dog after a Greek god.

Blame it on my need for comfort and happiness after the earthquake, or just the over-the-top cuteness of those pups, but despite Zeus' demeanor, we found ourselves back at Stacy's place. After some more puppy interaction, we settled on a female named Wednesday. The litter had not been named for days of the week, but after characters from the old Addams Family television series. There was a Pugsley and a Morticia, although I'm not sure whether they'd gone so far as to name a pup Cousin It. We paid, received a certificate that declared Wednesday to be 25% wolf, and drove off with C.C. at the wheel and Wednesday lying quietly in my lap.

As block after frosty suburban block rolled by, we laughed and chatted about the puppies' antics. Wednesday had been one of the more reticent of the bunch, hanging back and regarding us suspiciously as the others pups frolicked around us. My heartstrings have always been easily tugged by shy and frightened dogs, so the choice wasn't surprising. At the opposite end of the puppy behavior spectrum, there had been a male who had practically begged to be noticed. He'd jumped and pawed at us, wiggled joyfully as we'd petted him, and practically levitated from sheer excitement. We kept talking about him, smiling and laughing about his ploys for attention. Suddenly the conversation came to an abrupt halt. We exchanged a significant look—and turned the car around.

Stacy was happy to switch Wednesday for the pup who turned out to be…Fester. *Fester!* As in Uncle Fester. And, what an infected wound does. I couldn't imagine calling across a grassy expanse, "Fester, come!" The name would definitely be history as soon as we could think of something better. With the frisky, now-nameless pup in tow, we set off to make arrangements for the three of us to fly back to California.

We took the puppy to a nearby veterinarian and obtained a wellness check and health certificate for travel. A size small crate would contain him safely for the flight. Wanting to extend our cuddle time as long as possible, we held off crating the pup until we reached the airport. This might not have been the best plan. At the terminal, we discovered that he wouldn't fit through the crate door. Even at eight weeks, he was big-boned and weighed sixteen pounds. In desperation, with our flight time looming, we unscrewed the connectors and lifted the plastic top of the crate, put the puppy in, and then re-attached the top. One look at the way he filled the crate, fur poking crazily out in every direction, told us we'd have to find another solution, and quickly. Fortunately, the airline was able to swap us for a medium-sized crate. We were off!

Back in L.A., we renamed the mega-puppy Mojo, after the Doors lyrics-cum-anagram "Mr. Mojo Risin'." Mojo—or Mojo Potato Dog, as I called him in sillier times—had an amazing zest for life that shined through his every action. He'd inhale his food and then look for more; he once managed to get into a forty-pound sack of kibble and eat his way through a quarter of the bag before being caught. He wouldn't just chase a ball, he'd hunt it down and disembowel it. Stuffed toys feared for their lives.

One day when Mojo was a few months old, he ran full-bore through a dog door that was set into a slim glass panel. As he bolted out to the yard, he ended up wearing the entire panel around his waist. We might have been angry if we hadn't been laughing so hard. But Mojo had a softer side as well. He'd practically melt at softly spoken words or gentle petting, and tummy rubs sent him into in a state of transcendental bliss. Everything he did, he did 200%.

That wild puppy passion also translated to his play with Soko. He would jump on her with his miniature tank of a body and, with puppy-powered gusto, grab mouthfuls of her fur in an attempt to wrestle her to the ground. Soko, being the tolerant, sweet, submissive dog that she was, allowed him to do pretty much as he pleased. While that might sound lovely, it did nothing to teach him manners or how to play nicely with other dogs.

As Mojo matured, it became obvious that there was a problem. What had at first appeared to be a slight limp had, by the age of six months, morphed into a painful condition where his right leg dragged behind him with every step. X-rays revealed a hip socket so shallow that it barely surrounded the rounded head of the bone. All efforts at training and socialization were put on hold as Mojo underwent surgery and then a lengthy recovery process. Though the breeder denied any knowledge of hip dysplasia in the lines, she offered to swap Mojo for another puppy. But by now he was our child, and we'd no sooner have "swapped him out" than any parent would exchange their human offspring.

Thankfully, Mojo never developed the attitude of Thor or Zeus toward people. He wasn't exactly dog-aggressive, either, but he was what could best be described as dog-obnoxious. At the park, he'd chase down some poor, unsuspecting dog, and radiate bluff and bluster until the dog ended up on his back with Mojo standing over him, exuding a sort of proud glee. But as happy as the game seemed to make him, it was not acceptable behavior. Something had to be done.

I wasn't yet a professional trainer. Sure, I had done some training in Brooklyn and more in L.A., but it had never been my actual career. It seemed like a good time to get serious. I began to assist a man named Kyle in group training classes. Kyle lived way out in the desert, where he bred and trained wolfdogs. I woke up at four a.m. every Saturday and drove two hours to his training center. There, in a large field, ten sleepy people and their dogs would practice military-style drills as Kyle barked out orders: "Left! Forward! Stop! Sit your dogs! Right turn! Right! Right!" There was also the ever-present "Dammit, stop coddling that dog!" that could be elicited from Kyle simply by an owner talking kindly to their dog. Kyle was a nice enough guy when he wasn't teaching, but on the field, he was a drillmaster. My former experience as a competitive gymnast allowed me to excel at the precision footwork he demanded, but I was uncomfortable with the sharp, violent corrections administered to the dogs via metal choke chains. Oh, I had great timing. I gave corrections properly. And I got results. Still, something just felt inherently *wrong* in the way we were treating the dogs.

I brought Soko and Mojo along to the classes so I could practice with them as well. Naturally, Kyle coached me on how to fix Mojo's reactivity toward other dogs. This entailed walking him past the other students' dogs, who were tethered at intervals to the chain link fence. Whenever Mojo barked or lunged, I was to correct him by giving a hard yank of the choke chain while yelling in his face. Although I assumed Kyle knew more than I did about dog behavior, the exercise made *me* cringe. I couldn't help it. Mojo stopped lunging immediately whenever he was corrected, but I was being far from kind to my dog, and I worried about the effect it might be having on him emotionally. Still, I didn't have the knowledge, experience, or confidence to stand up to Kyle, especially in front of the other students.

The weekly training sessions continued, and I reluctantly went along with the program—that is, until the day I saw something truly terrible. As the students sat and watched, Kyle worked with a five-month-old puppy. He issued a command. The pup didn't comply. Kyle loomed over the pup and barked the command more loudly. The puppy snapped at him. Suddenly, four tiny paws flailed wildly as the dog gasped, his air supply cut off by the choke chain from which Kyle was hanging him. Urine dribbled down the puppy's leg. Kyle, satisfied that the willful pup had submitted, dropped him back to the ground. The class ended a few minutes later. I left and never returned.

Mojo was, as modern trainers refer to it, my "cross-over dog." He helped me to learn that there are better, gentler ways to train that are just as effective. I was soon able to replace yelling, jerking, and other punishments with praise, treats, and affection. I taught Mojo what was expected, set him up to succeed, and then rewarded him instead of giving him inadequate information and then correcting him for mistakes. I also taught him a variety of tricks, including the very cute Say Your Prayers, and Turn Out the Lights. I loved secretly practicing tricks with Mojo during the days, and then surprising C.C. when he came home from work. One night, C.C. and I were lounging on the couch watching television. I casually turned to Mojo and said, "Turn out the lights." C.C. looked at me as if thinking, *So now you're calling me by the dog's name?* Mojo padded up the stairs to the light switch, hit it with his nose, and plunged us into darkness. By the dim glow of the television I could see the amazed look on C.C.'s face. I was so proud of my boy! All of our practicing had been worth it, and it had been fun, besides. I finally had the kind of training relationship with my dog that I could feel good about. Mojo and I were both much happier, and by using gentle methods, we were eventually able to improve his behavior around other dogs. I never did get over the guilt about the harsh way I'd treated Mojo early on in the name of training. I vowed to spend the rest of his life making it up to him.

~ * ~ * ~ * ~ * ~ * ~ * ~ * ~ * ~ * ~ * ~ * ~ *

We decided to stay in California after all. But although our rented home was nice enough, we longed to be out of the city. After a month of searching, we found a ranch-style home in a rural area forty-five minutes outside Los Angeles. We chose the location because it was close to the wolf rescue I had gotten involved with—more on that later. Mojo and Soko accompanied us for peaceful walks down quiet dirt roads, tails wagging happily as they pounced into the brush after rabbits and squirrels, and explored the weeds and plants that managed to thrive in the harsh desert landscape. The screaming of sirens had been replaced by the howls of coyotes, and the sweet scents of sage and rosemary wafted from the surrounding hills. We all loved it.

C.C. and Soko didn't mind the heat, but Mojo and I begged to differ. Every summer, Mojo and I took refuge in the cool, air-conditioned house as outdoor temperatures hovered in the low hundreds, sometimes soaring as high as 115. I'd take the dogs for walks and run errands in the relative cool of the morning, and then spend the rest of the day working from home. I had begun writing books almost by default. I'd been part of an online discussion group about wolfdogs, and I quickly found myself spending two to three hours a day answering emails from people requesting help. Since the problems were common ones, I ended up giving the same advice over and over. And so, the idea of creating a book was born. That way, I thought, I could give a helpful hint or two and then refer people to the book. I proposed to a small group of knowledgeable wolf people that we each write a chapter. The response was the same across the board: "Great idea! ...Let us know when it's done." And so I began to write my first book, *Living with Wolfdogs*.

Mojo would lie on the cool tiles of my home office as I sat at the computer. If I worked too long he'd pad over and sit facing me, place a paw on my leg, and give me a meaningful look that said, *Isn't it about time to take a break and rub my tummy?* He was always right. Tummy rubbing was, hands-down, our favorite activity. I'd sit there singing nonsensical songs, blissed out and not caring how ridiculous I sounded. Mojo would writhe on his back, luxuriating in the glow of love. My favorite tummy rubbing song had grown out of Simon and Garfunkel's "Love Me Like a Rock." I'd sing, *"Cause my mommy loves me/She loves me/She get down her knees and rub me/She r-u-u-b me like a dog."* What can I say? It worked for us.

Time passes much too quickly, and all too soon our dogs were seniors. With age, Mojo had mellowed. Soko, unfortunately, had developed degenerative myelopathy, a disease that causes progressive nerve damage to the spine and hind end. She was left "knuckling under"—dragging her knuckles on the ground—and was eventually barely able to walk. In 2006, with great sadness, we made the decision to euthanize her. She was thirteen. Mojo was eleven at the time, and all too soon it became apparent that he had developed the very same disease. Soko had been a purebred German Shepherd, and DM isn't uncommon in the breed. But Mojo being afflicted as well was a terrible shock. Soko's symptoms had come on so quickly and so late in her life that there hadn't been much we could do. In an effort to do absolutely everything possible for Mojo, I launched into a full-fledged research campaign.

There were supplements. There were pills. I did energy healing and massage. And we drove an hour each way every Saturday to a canine rehabilitation facility. There, a wonderful, kind therapist would stretch and massage Mojo, and guide him through exercises that included balancing his hind legs on a wooden wobble board, and walking on a treadmill in a water-filled tank. It took him a while to get accustomed to the water therapy. He never did grow to like it, but I knew the way to that boy's heart. It was, as the cliché goes, through his stomach. I stood at the front of the water tank and encouraged him to keep walking by dangling a long, peanut butter-filled wooden spoon a few inches in front of his face. The first few times I tried it he quickened his pace, snagged a lick of peanut butter, and then went into such a peanut-butter-induced haze that he forgot to keep walking. It was hard not to laugh as he glided backward with a surprised, comical look on his face, only to remember seconds later to start walking again. While all of the supplements and therapies didn't reverse the disease process, they did appear to slow the physical deterioration.

Some dogs, like people, become crankier as they get older. Mojo got sweeter. He'd always loved affection, but he now seemed to enjoy physical closeness even more. He lived for the moments when C.C. would walk through the front door after work. After their joyous greeting, C.C. would massage Mojo from head to tail, effectively turning him into a lump of jelly. Mojo and I had our own special times, too. On warm afternoons I would lie on the floor spooning his long body with mine, and pet him in long, soothing strokes as I whispered into his ear and kissed the warm, soft fur on top of his head. At other times he would lie on his side and I'd lay my head on his deep barrel of a chest, just listening to his heart beating, feeling a deep gratitude that he was still with us. Of all the wonderful memories, those quiet, intimate moments are the ones I cherish the most.

In 2008, Mojo was fourteen. On the Friday leading up to Memorial Day, I was working at home when he began to pace and whine. He vomited a little bit of white, foamy-looking stuff. I immediately called the emergency vet, as my regular vet was already gone for the weekend. The receptionist, after consulting with the vet on duty, told me to fast Mojo for twelve hours. Ten minutes later C.C. came home from work and I told him what had happened. As we were speaking, Mojo went outside and spewed a huge amount of white foam. We immediately rushed him to the emergency clinic.

There was only one vet on duty, and she was currently trying to save another dog who was having a very bad start to his weekend. We waited. Five minutes. Ten. Fifteen. I walked out to the receptionist and insisted that someone take a look at Mojo right away. A tech came and took him to a back room, saying that he would ask the vet to examine him. A few minutes later, the vet appeared and told us that Mojo had bloated. I was floored. Bloat had never even entered my mind. After all, he hadn't been dry heaving, a common sign of bloat; he'd actually been vomiting. But he had definitely bloated, with gastric torsion and all. We were told that if emergency surgery wasn't performed immediately, he would die. The receptionist came in and quoted us a fee that was incredibly high. And, she warned, the aftercare was going to be very difficult. *And* Mojo was fourteen. His chances of making it through the surgery were 50/50. Were we sure we wanted them to try to save him? I looked at her and said, "Get someone in there and save my dog."

It was a very long, difficult weekend, but thankfully, Mojo pulled through. The first seventy-two hours after bloat surgery are critical, as many dogs develop heart arrhythmias during that time and die. Did I mention how long and difficult the weekend was? The following weeks involved, as promised, plenty of aftercare, but as C.C. said, "He's the Mighty Mojo Man. He's a fighter."

Although Mojo recovered fully from the bloat, he was having trouble getting to his feet and his gait was shaky. Because we had replaced the wall-to-wall carpeting with tile when we first moved in, we were now faced with too-slippery flooring. We went shopping for carpet remnants and ended up placing large, mismatched pieces all over the house. It looked as though a rug salesman had exploded in there! C.C. built a small, carpet-covered ramp to bridge the foyer and living room so Mojo wouldn't have to stumble down the two small steps. He also built a large outdoor ramp that sported a flat deck-like top that allowed Mojo to exit the dog door on to a flat surface rather than having to navigate an immediate downward slope. Indoors or out, we employed a sling with handles to help him stand up and get around. By this time, his weight had gone from a healthy 120 pounds all the way down to ninety, but it was still a challenge to support him as walking became more of a struggle. Knuckling under from the DM, he now had to wear special booties to prevent his toes from becoming bloodied as he dragged them along. You might assume that Mojo was miserable. But rather than becoming depressed by this state of affairs, he retained an amazing lust for life. He continued to enthusiastically eat his food and anything else he could get his paws on, and still gloried in receiving petting and attention. He clearly still wanted to be here.

That September, I had a speaking engagement in England. I absolutely did not want to leave Mojo, but I couldn't cancel since the arrangements had been made a year before and over eighty attendees had already paid. So I made the ten-hour flight, spoke for two days, and then immediately turned around and flew home. As exhausted as I was, I could see that Mojo was not doing well. Two mornings later, he woke up and refused his breakfast. The light in his eyes was dim, and his whole demeanor announced that he'd had enough. The crushing weight of that final decision was upon us. It was time.

At the clinic, the veterinarian left the room to allow us a few last precious moments with our baby. C.C. is not a man given easily to tears, but he cried his heart out. I did the same. All too soon the vet returned. As he injected Mojo with the fluid that would cause his loyal heart to stop beating, Mojo looked at me. With my face up to his, I gazed softly and deeply into his soulful, brown eyes. I said, "I love you, buddy. I'll see you on the other side."

*3*

# Into the Desert

After Mojo passed, getting another dog was unthinkable. *I'll just be with the grief,* I decided grimly. *I'll work through it.* And I had plenty of time to do just that. I'd fashioned my life into a model that allowed me to work from home so as to share as much of Mojo's precious remaining time as possible. Now I was left with a daily procession of endless, empty hours. The house that had always been peaceful and quiet was now *too* quiet.

Each morning, I would wake up crying. I'd go into my office and attempt to work, but would instead end up sinking down onto the dark carpet, rendered inert by the crushing weight of sorrow. How was it possible that my buddy, my Mojo Potato Dog, wasn't lying next to me, looking up at me with those big, sweet brown eyes? All I wanted was to stroke his long, soft fur one more time. At the end of each seemingly endless day, I'd cry myself to sleep.

Despite my resolution to deal with my emotions, I was drowning in wave after wave of grief with no lifeboat in sight. Alarming amounts of hair began to show up in the shower drain and in my hairbrush. My throat had become so sore from crying that I came perilously close to losing my voice entirely. My eyes were perpetually puffy and red. I looked like hell, and for the first time in my life I just didn't care. I finally understood why some people choose to get another dog right away when their dog passes; otherwise, it's simply unbearable.

Here's what no one tells you: grief makes you stupid. I burned my hand on the stove. Twice. I banged myself black and blue on furniture corners that I knew perfectly well were there. I went out when I absolutely had to, but I really had no business driving. It was as though a cocoon of cotton had been spun around my brain, and the fuzzy insulation kept me from thinking too hard. But just as I would begin to fall into a comforting haze, a stabbing reminder would jolt me back to reality. There was breakfast time, when I had always shared my cereal banana with Mojo. He'd sit there with a happy, expectant grin, tail wagging, secure in the knowledge that our familiar routine would yield a piece of the yummy yellow stuff after I'd portioned some out for myself. It would be a few slices for me, and then one for Mojo. Now, with him gone, I'd cut a few slices of banana and then catch myself with arm outstretched, a piece of banana hovering in empty space.

My daily routine had been built around making sure Mojo was okay, and spending as much time with him as possible. Now, when I was out doing errands, it would still occur to me to get home to check on him. Those neural pathways in the brain can be little highways to hell. That microsecond delay before I realized that rushing home was no longer necessary was a killer.

~ * ~ * ~ * ~ * ~ * ~ * ~ * ~ * ~ * ~ * ~ * ~ *

Time can be a creeping, relentless enemy, but it also bestows the gift of healing. As the months passed, I began to dip a tentative toe back into the stream of life. Sure, I still fell apart here and there. A million little things reminded me of Mojo. But, gradually, I began to be able to look back on the happy times without the accompanying sadness.

A year after Mojo's passing, I couldn't take it any more. I *had* to have a dog. C.C. reluctantly agreed. He would have been perfectly happy to remain dogless—and thereby dog-hairless, six a.m. dog walk-less, and less all the other things that stressed him out about having a dog. But he knew how much it meant to me, and it was sweetly characteristic of him that he just wanted me to be happy. I was in dire need of some happy.

"How about getting a puppy?" he suggested helpfully.

"A *puppy*?" I was taken aback. "I want to *rescue* a dog! Besides, I don't want to be up in the middle of the night with a puppy, and have to start all over with the socialization, the housebreaking…you know, all the stuff that goes along with it."

"Sure," he agreed, "But you know what happens when you adopt an adult dog. They all come with baggage."

"Well, so do we," I responded pointedly, "but it doesn't stop us from getting into new relationships."

With a sigh, C.C. turned to walk away. Over his shoulder, he said, "You're going to look back on this and wish you'd gotten a puppy."

Determined to save a life, I scoured shelters near and far, searched online adoption sites, networked, read bulletin boards in pet stores, and pored over newspaper ads. But for all of my efforts, I just couldn't seem to find the right dog. Part of the problem was that a lot of the dogs I was attracted to looked too much like Mojo. As tempting as that was, I knew it would be a mistake. Also, the breeds I gravitated toward were not generally the most easy-going, happy-go-lucky types. Rottweilers, German Shepherds, Malamutes—yes, all the breeds in Mojo's genetic makeup—would catch my eye. But each candidate, upon further examination, seemed to have aggression issues or other major behavior problems.

A friend who lived in upstate New York was not only a talented author and canine behavior specialist, but a long-time breeder of German Shepherds. She produced large, beautiful dogs, but more importantly, they had lovely, stable temperaments—a characteristic that seems to be in short supply in many German Shepherd lines these days. She was very careful about qualifying potential owners, and rightfully so. She mentioned that one of her dogs was expecting a litter, and offered me the chance to purchase one of the pups. I was honored, and actually considered the idea. But in the end, I stuck by my commitment to rescue an adult dog.

Countless friends and colleagues, eager to help, asked what type of dog I was looking for. The trouble was, I really couldn't say. I knew what I *didn't* want. People assume that trainers are the perfect candidates to take on dogs with severe problems, and in a way, they're right. But trainers need a break, too! Being a professional, I knew better than anyone the time and effort major behavior issues can take to fix. It only made me more determined to avoid them. I'd gone through thirteen years of Soko's fear issues, and Mojo's reactivity toward other dogs. In addition, I most definitely did not want a wild and crazy adolescent. That unbridled enthusiasm for life and super high activity level might have been just fine in my younger days, but somehow I didn't get a warm and fuzzy feeling when I thought of bringing a teenager into our peaceful home.

As with any other relationship, I felt confident that I'd know it when the right one came along. Months passed, and I kept hoping and searching. Rescue groups had been circulating my email address and I was bombarded with photos on a daily basis. Still, despite the fact that I was open to either sex, a reasonable age range, and a variety of breeds...nothing. Then, on December 18, Mojo's birthday, I was sitting at the computer performing my daily scouring of the Petfinder website. Suddenly, there she was! A beautiful, two-year-old female northern breed mix who'd been brought in as a stray. It was her. I *knew* it. The shelter was an hour away. I dropped everything and drove into the desert.

*4*

# The Miniature Christmas Wolf

County animal shelters are often overcrowded and understaffed, and this one was no exception. In each of three brick buildings, row after row of pens held dogs who were crammed together so tightly that some had to step over each other to reach the food and water buckets. Urine and feces were spread over concrete floors, and the stench of hopelessness hung in the air.

I walked sadly down the aisles of the dank grey building that housed the females, knowing that many of those wonderful, deserving dogs would never leave the shelter alive. I searched in the gloom for the bright little face I'd seen online. The photo hadn't shown her full body, but still, I felt sure I'd be able to spot her. Five minutes later, I had walked through the entire building twice. None of the dogs resembled her. A ball of dread began to form in the pit of my stomach. Had she already been adopted out? Had there been an error on the website? Or had something unspeakably worse happened? Finally, a kindly staff person informed me that the third building held both male and female dogs, and pointed me toward it.

I found her right away. She looked just as soft, and just as sweet as she had in the photo. Her amber eyes held a warmth and a light that defied her harsh surroundings. The black eyeliner-like rim around her eyes gave them a lovely, ethereal glow. She looked up at me with an expression that could only be described as delight, and immediately pressed the length of her thin body against the metal bars. Kneeling, I stroked the long, silky fur that fell across her back in bands of cream and grey. She leaned against the bars in an apparent attempt to melt right through them. That was it. I was in love. Just then, a friendly volunteer appeared, and I asked if we could bring the dog to a getting-to-know-you area. The shelter had three spaces designated for meet and greets. Two were tiny dog runs with a small bench added for human comfort, and the last was a larger chain link enclosure where dogs could stretch their legs and run around a bit. Luckily, the enclosure was available.

I sat on the bench, not wanting to interfere as the dog sniffed around the perimeter of the enclosure, clearly thrilled to be out of the cramped pen. She was on the small side, weighing forty pounds or so. All the dogs and wolfdogs we'd had over the years had been large and sturdily built. Most had been pushy brutes, at least when I'd first gotten them. This little girl was almost dainty in comparison. She moved in a sort of gliding walk-run, as though her body were suspended from wires. It gave the illusion of limbs moving smoothly through space without the burden of weight. The impression of a wild, exotic animal would have been complete had it not been for the tail. The spectacular, cream-colored curly plume was perched on her rear like a royal proclamation. It looked almost as though it belonged on another dog. But instead of seeming ungainly, it only enhanced her beauty.

The other interesting feature of her body was the tongue; it was spotted. I don't mean it had a dark patch—I mean, it had small, dark purple blotches all over, giving her an almost comical look whenever she opened her mouth. Most people assume that spots on a dog's tongue indicate Chow in the mix. In reality, there are over 30 breeds that can have spotted tongues, including purebred German Shepherds, Golden Retrievers, and Siberian Huskies. The unusual tongue and tail didn't cause the dog to lose her exotic looks entirely, though, because a passing animal control officer smiled and commented, "She looks like a miniature wolf." I smiled, patted the bench, and called to my lovely mini-lupine. She glided over and, with effortless grace, jumped up next to me. We cuddled together, happy and content. She licked my face. I wondered how soon I could drag C.C. to the shelter to see her.

Thirty minutes later, a volunteer had placed my dog back in her pen. Yes, in my mind she was already *my* dog. I asked when she would be available for adoption. After checking the cage card and consulting the computer, a front office staffer reported that the dog had been impounded two days earlier as a stray. Because she had a microchip, an attempt to contact the owners had been made. My heart sank. *Owners?* Of course, I knew it was possible that any dog there might have an owner, but somehow—perhaps because the volunteer had been allowed to take the dog out for a visit—I had assumed she was up for adoption. (I later found out the volunteer was not technically supposed to have taken her out, but I'm forever grateful that she did.) A call had been placed but the phone number was out of service, so a letter had been sent. If no one turned up to claim the dog within ten business days, I could adopt her. If I wished, I could file a Contract to Adopt, which would give me first rights if the owners didn't show. Who knew my feet could move so fast? I practically flew to the front office, darting sideways glances at other potential adopters, intent on heading them off at the pass.

The next day, I returned to the shelter with C.C. in tow. He and the dog took to each other immediately. My girl was no fool. She flirted and played up to him, planting kisses all over his face, efficiently reducing him to a fountain of adjectives: "She's beautiful," "So gentle," and "Really sweet." For all of his hesitation about getting another dog, he had to agree that this one was special.

Every few days, I drove to the shelter. My soon-to-be fur-kid would see me approaching with the volunteer, and do a head to toe happy dance in anticipation of our visit. I'd sit with her in the enclosure for as long as they'd let me. I tried to get her to chase a ball. She had no interest, but she would chase me around if I encouraged her. Once, another volunteer passed by and made a comment similar to that of the first animal control officer. "Oh!" she exclaimed. "She looks like a miniature wolf!" I suppose in a way she did. The mini-wolf and I spent lots of time snuggling together on the wooden bench. I put my lips close to her small, furred ears and whispered about the sage-filled mountains, plush dog beds, tummy rubs, and love that awaited her.

One day I arrived at the shelter to find that my girl's usual pen mate had been replaced by a German Shepherd. As my dog approached to greet me, the Shepherd jumped on her. A fight broke out. My mini-wolf was on her back, scrapping mightily, holding her own against the beastly offender. I looked around frantically for a staff member or volunteer, but there was no one in sight. I yelled, hoping to startle the dogs out of the skirmish. No dice. I looked for a water hose but couldn't find one. I kicked at the iron bars hard and yelled again. Still, nothing. Finally, I ran outside the kennel building and found a worker who followed me all too slowly back inside, where the dogs were *still* fighting. He opened the gallows gate that separated the inside from the outer part of the run, and managed to lock the Shepherd outside. I thanked him and expressed concern that the dogs might fight again once they were allowed back together. He said he couldn't promise anything, but he'd try to move one of the dogs to a different pen.

At home, I worried incessantly. *Would the dogs fight? Would the owners show up?* At the least, a disconnected phone meant they'd moved without bothering to have the information on the dog's microchip updated. *What sorts of owners were those?* I wondered uncharitably. I mean, who *wouldn't* have turned up at the shelter by now, frantically searching for this amazing sweetheart of a dog? I tried very hard to maintain the attitude that if there were extenuating circumstances and this dog really was better off with her owners, that their showing up would be the best thing for everyone. But in my heart of hearts, I desperately hoped no one would come.

The shelter was closed for almost a week over the Christmas holidays. I hated not being able to see my girl, and I agonized about the owners turning up as soon as the shelter re-opened. I tried not to worry about her getting into another fight, but the images of the last one haunted my thoughts. Worst of all, I feared that an error might be made and she'd be euthanized; sadly, it's been known to happen. It was a very long week. Finally, on December 30th, I drove to the shelter, gave the front office the impound number, and told them I wanted to adopt the dog. The clerk located the records. As she processed the paperwork, she commented that the dog had been in the shelter four times previously. *Four times?* Had she been brought in as a stray each time? Was there a frustrated owner who kept having to bail her out after yet another great escape? Or had there been four different owners? No information was available, other than that she'd been impounded and then adopted out a few months earlier. I didn't care. "Say goodbye," I told the officer, "because you're never going to see this dog again."

~ * ~ * ~ * ~ * ~ * ~ * ~ * ~ * ~ * ~ * ~ * ~ * ~ *

The bouncy ball of fluff rode happily behind the metal partition of my Jeep, excited to look out the windows and breathe the fresh air. I still hadn't come up with a suitable name for her. The only piece of information the shelter clerk had was that at some point the dog's name had been "Regina." I tried calling the dog by that name, but she didn't respond. I didn't blame her. As we drove along the freeway, I thought, *I need a name that's a bit wild, something that reflects the mountains and nature...* Just then, I passed a freeway sign for an exit called Sierra Highway. That was it! Sierra! I smiled. It was perfect.

The only worrisome behavior I'd noticed during our getting-to-know-you sessions at the shelter had been a blatant attempt to escape through a small hole at the bottom of the enclosure's chain link fence. The first time she'd tried to squirm through I'd stopped her, made sure she didn't have further access to the area, and notified the shelter staff of the problem. It was understandable that a dog would want out, but, combined with her impound history, it also made me wonder whether I'd have an escape artist on my hands.

Once home, I walked Sierra directly to the enclosed area in back of the house and removed her leash. The space wasn't so much a yard as a rambling, paved area we'd enclosed with chain link immediately upon buying the house. She immediately began a thorough inspection of the perimeter. She padded along with an intent, deliberate focus, sniffing down low and gazing up at the top of the fence, sizing it all up. *Yep,* I thought, *that's why you've been in the shelter four times. You're Houdini in fur.* I would soon find out that wasn't the only reason.

5

# Double Crazy Legs

Watching the self-appointed Fence Inspector at work, it became all too clear that our first order of business had to be to raise the height of the fence. Gus, a fifty-something, laid back local, had originally installed the six-foot-tall chain link. He had northern breed dogs of his own, so he wasn't at all surprised at my request to extend the fence height to eight feet and to add lean-ins. Lean-ins, those angled overhangs that sit atop chain link with fencing material (or sometimes barbed wire!) strung between them, help to keep zoo animals in their enclosures. From the animal's vantage point, it looks insurmountable. Insurmountable sounded good to me.

Unfortunately, Gus was booked up and wouldn't be able to come by for another two weeks. So, with only the possibly-not-adequate fencing in place, every time Sierra went out back, one of us had to go with her. For all of our togetherness at the shelter, she hadn't truly bonded with me yet, and I couldn't take the chance that she'd run off. We escorted her out back on a thirty-foot long line multiple times daily so she could have room to do her business, but couldn't jump the fence. I can't say it was all that much fun. Even though we're in southern California, January in the desert can still be pretty darned cold. I'm not talking about a wimpy fifty degrees kind of cold, either; I mean water freezing in the pipes cold.

It quickly became obvious that Sierra had lived indoors before. She was housebroken, and treated the plush dog beds like long-lost friends. With a shudder, I thought about how she must have hated those cold, damp, concrete shelter floors. Happily, household sounds like those made by the microwave and the vacuum cleaner didn't frighten her. I was relieved. Because we didn't know whether she'd be destructive when left alone, I planned to have Sierra sleep in a crate. I instructed C.C. that if she whined or barked for a bit, to ignore it. It would eventually stop. Dog trainers and parents have used this logic for eons, and it works. Usually, that is. Sierra began to whine and cry in a way that suggested not frustration at being enclosed, but a complete and utter panic. It was bloodcurdling, and it made *me* want to panic. I couldn't leave her in there. I thought about tethering her to something, but instinctively felt that she'd panic in that situation as well. In the end, we left her loose in the house with the dog door shut. We closed all the interior doors. C.C. had long ago deemed our bedroom, along with his music studio (a.k.a. the third bedroom) off-limits to dogs anyway. I put away anything within easy reach and hoped for the best. The next morning, we were pleasantly surprised to find that absolutely nothing had been destroyed or even moved. Sierra was lying contentedly on the dog bed, looking completely at home. She gazed up at us, her amber eyes sparkling, mouth open in a relaxed smile. Sweetness radiated from her like light. I thanked the Powers That Be that we had found such a wonderful dog.

On Day Two, we began obedience training. Sierra already knew Sit and quickly learned Down. But something disconcerting happened when we began to practice Stay. When I made a small motion with my hand in the "halt" position as a cue to remain in place, Sierra acted as though I was about to strike her. Her ears flattened. Her eyes became squinted slits. She cringed. Then she shut down completely, not moving, unwilling to even look at me. This "learned helplessness" isn't uncommon in dogs who have been trained with an overly firm hand or treated harshly. It's as though they're afraid to do *anything* for fear of being wrong and incurring the human's wrath. My heart ached for her. How could anyone raise a hand to this beautiful, gentle creature? I tried using as small and mild a version of the hand signal as possible, but since it still worried her, I switched to a soft verbal cue instead. She seemed much more relaxed, and participated willingly in the exercise.

We soon fell into a routine. On weekdays, upon my appearance in the bedroom doorway, Sierra would race over to the couch and jump up to wait for me, tail wagging in eager anticipation. She'd learned quickly that as long as the large Native American blanket we used as a couch cover was in place, she was allowed up. I would smile and head sleepily to the couch for our morning petting session. She luxuriated in tummy rubs and ear scratches, and would lie on her back with one or both of her front legs thrust straight up into the air, her head tilted back, clearly loving life. C.C. and I took to calling these comical positions "Crazy Legs" and "Double Crazy Legs." "Look, you've got Double Crazy legs," C.C. would point out, grinning as he left for work. After the cuddle session, Sierra and I would jump into the Jeep and drive to the local park. I was thrilled to discover that she was friendly toward the dogs we encountered, and absolutely adored people.

Naturally, Sierra was always leashed in public. With her history, I was adamant that she would never be loose, at least until she was extremely well trained. At home, we no longer left the long line on during back yard outings, but we still accompanied her. This was an inconvenience, since she frequently wanted to go outside and I never knew whether it was because she really had to *go* or if she just wanted to explore the scintillating scents of the critters that lived in the foothills and the crevices under our storage sheds. But out we went.

One skill Sierra hadn't had a problem learning from the start was the recall—come when called—and we practiced it multiple times daily. I knew she was a runner, after all, and if the worst happened, I wanted a shot at getting her back. I had meant what I'd said to the shelter staff about never seeing her again. We started the exercises with very little distance between us, but Sierra was soon happily racing to me from inside the house as I called her from outside, and vice versa. She learned quickly, was highly responsive, and seemed to enjoy the fun, reward-based training. Other than the worry she displayed now and then when trying to learn something new, she seemed like a wonderfully well-adjusted dog whose confidence was slowly growing. Could it be that I had finally ended up with a dog who didn't have any major behavior issues?

Gus, the fencing guru, had been delayed by a job that had gone longer than expected, so it wasn't until three weeks later that he came by to give us an estimate. By that time, we'd stopped accompanying Sierra outdoors. We secretly watched through the bedroom window as she explored, and she'd never shown even a glimmer of interest in going over or under the fence. She was, however, constantly alert to the scents of the creatures that lived outside. She would patrol the area, sniffing the ground and scenting the air above. Then she'd go rigid, a hard, focused gleam in her eye. She would slink along with a slow, stalking motion, then lie down and wait for the unsuspecting lizard or mouse to venture from its hiding place. The girl had infinite patience and lightning-fast reflexes. We began to find an unsettling number of small, dead creatures in back of the house. At least we were now comfortable leaving her alone with outside access when we were at home, and also when we were gone for short periods. Still, it sure would be nice to have that higher fencing in place.

Finally, Gus arrived. Sierra greeted him like a long-lost friend, licking his face and wriggling happily as he petted her. Like so many others who met her, Gus immediately fell prey to her charms. C.C. and I went back indoors, leaving her to supervise the fencing pro as he took measurements and made calculations. A short time later he returned with Sierra dancing happily along by his side. The job seemed doable, he reported, lean-ins and all. He'd call or email with the estimate shortly. We waved as he got back into his old Ford pickup truck and drove off.

The following day, C.C. left for work and I began the usual morning chores. With Sierra lazing on the living room dog bed, I finished what needed doing in the house and then left for the post office. By the time I got through the line and returned home, I'd been gone just under an hour. It was longer than I had ever left Sierra alone, but I wasn't concerned. I entered the house, expecting her to greet me at the door. Instead, I was greeted by silence. That was odd. "Sierra," I called out. Nothing. *Hmm*, I thought, *she must be out back stalking something.* I walked out the back door and down the dog ramp, and looked around. I didn't see her anywhere. My heart began to pound faster. "Sierra! *Sierra?*" I called. No answer. I went back indoors to see whether I'd somehow locked her inside one of the rooms when I'd closed all the doors. Nope. Now frantic, I ran back outside and checked behind the storage sheds. We'd set up barriers to prevent her from getting behind them, but with her agility skills, I thought she might still be able to get past them. I checked everywhere, but she was nowhere to be found. I ran back inside and, with tears streaming down my face, called C.C. at work. "She's gone!" I cried.

After I managed to convey what had happened, C.C. promised to make the twenty-minute drive home right away to help search. I hung up and ran to the front door with the intention of jumping into the Jeep to drive up and down our road calling for Sierra. But something stopped me.

Instead, I stood on the front porch and, facing nothing but the mountains in front of me, yelled, "Sierra, come!" in the high, happy voice I'd used during our many training sessions. I kept it up, and even added some "Good girl coming to me!" for good measure. I kept up the "keep going" encouragement, as though I knew she was running toward me. Lo and behold, seconds later, there she was! That beautiful bundle of fur came flying over the mountain top, tail wagging, excited, and joyful at seeing me. Shocked, relieved, and more than a little joyful myself, I kept calling until she reached me and I was able to get her into the house. A shower of praise and hot dogs followed.

Once Sierra was safely indoors with the dog door shut and I'd called C.C. to give him the good news, I walked back outside to figure out how she had escaped. It was possible that she'd climbed the fence and gone over the chain link, as it hadn't yet been extended. But I remembered that when I'd first seen her scope out her new digs, she'd paid an awful lot of attention to the bottom of the fence line. That, combined with the way she had attempted to squirm through the fence at the shelter, made me suspect that jumping wasn't her preferred mode of escape. As it turned out, I was right. Upon careful inspection of the perimeter, I discovered that Gus had, unbeknownst to us, removed a small piece of wood we had wired to the bottom of a chain link panel to cover a hole that had been there when we'd moved in. Surely he'd assumed the hole wasn't big enough for Sierra to slip through—but he was wrong. To test my theory, I opened the dog door and left Sierra in the house with access to the outdoors. I grabbed a leash, walked out the front door, and quickly ran around to the torn fence. Sure enough, there was Sierra, her body already halfway through the opening. Once free, she grinned at me, that spectacular tail wagging, as if to say, *Wasn't that fun?* Unable to suppress a smile, I attached the leash and walked her back inside, where she stayed while I wired the board back into place. Well, life certainly wasn't going to be dull with *this* dog around!

*6*

# Don't Leave Me

Once the new and improved fencing was in place, I could leave Sierra home alone with indoor-outdoor access. There were no more escape attempts, and no destruction or potty accidents, either. I could finally relax. I had, however, begun to notice a disconcerting behavior. Each time I returned home, Sierra was panting heavily. Since it was winter, I knew it wasn't heat-related. And the way she almost climbed up my leg to greet me had a frantic edge about it. The next day before I left the house, I set up a video camera. Forty-five minutes later I reviewed the footage. To say it was disturbing would be an understatement.

The video began with Sierra pacing continuously between the living room window and the French doors, both of which offered a view of the long, sloped driveway. Back and forth, back and forth she went, whimpering softly. As the pacing continued, the sound escalated to an intense whining, interspersed with short, high-pitched barks. It continued for ten minutes or so. To me, it seemed as though her distress went on forever. Then she began to howl. It was a mournful, pitiful sound that tore at my heart. Unable to watch the entire thing, I fast-forwarded, stopping and checking the footage periodically. The behavior had continued the entire time I was gone. No wonder she'd always been panting when I returned! The poor dog clearly had a case of separation anxiety. It wasn't surprising, either, given her history.

I immediately went into dog trainer mode. First, I rounded up all the products that had been helpful to my clients' dogs. There was DAP—Dog Appeasing Pheromone—which resembles a plug-in air freshener and emits a chemical copy of the pheromones released by lactating female dogs. The pheromones are, or course, comforting to puppies, but as it turns out, they're also comforting to adult dogs. The product had helped many of my clients' dogs with mild separation issues. After a few days' trial, though, I had to admit that it did nothing to ease Sierra's anxiety. I left music playing—and not just any music, either. This CD was psycho-acoustically designed to help dogs to relax. The *Through a Dog's Ear* series had proved helpful to many of my clients whose dogs needed calming. But while it might have soothed them, it didn't do a thing to calm this particular canine. The same went for each and every thing I tried; and believe me, I tried everything in the book. It seemed, though, that Sierra just hadn't read the book.

One staple of any separation treatment program is to leave the dog with something yummy to chew on when the owner is away. The more a dog is involved in chewing on something, or excavating treats from inside of something, the less likely he is to be spiraling out of control emotionally. My favorite standby is the Kong, a hard rubber snowman-shaped toy with a big hole at the bottom and a small one at the top. I've stuffed many a Kong in my day, and I felt certain I could concoct one that would keep Sierra busy while I was gone.

Unfortunately, I quickly discovered that Sierra wouldn't even *attempt* to get at the treats hidden inside, regardless of how easy I made it. The learned helplessness I'd seen during training sessions seemed to resurface when it came to trying anything in the excavation department. So I made it easier. I gave her bully sticks that she didn't have to do anything but chew. She still wasn't game. If it were simply a matter of her not eating while I was away, that would be understandable, as anorexia is a common symptom among dogs with separation issues. But she wouldn't even chew anything when I was home. What had happened to this dog? Had she never been given chew bones? Or had she been punished for chewing on things and was now afraid to try? Undaunted, I kept testing out one item after another. Finally, one day I placed a cup of Frosty Paws, an ice cream treat made for dogs, in front of her. To my great relief, she licked at it tentatively, and then with more interest.

Of course, a behavior protocol also had to be implemented. The idea was to teach Sierra, in very small increments, that being alone was okay. Many dogs who have separation anxiety are "Velcro dogs," sticking to their owner's side to the point of wanting to follow them everywhere, even into the bathroom. The usual protocol begins with the dog becoming accustomed to being separated from the owner while the owner is still in the house. But strangely, as long as Sierra knew I was at home, she preferred to be outside in back of the house. After all, that's where the mice and squirrels were! Without the typical clinginess issues, we were able to skip ahead in the protocol.

Pre-planned, brief separations would be necessary. I knew they had to be carried out carefully, with the duration of absences gradually lengthened. I also had to consider how Sierra would be managed when we weren't practicing. For example, how would I do a half-hour's worth of errands? What if I had a doctor's appointment or another place I *had* to be? Most people don't realize how challenging it is to live with a dog who has separation issues. Despite the fact that I'd helped many clients' dogs through it, I had never fully realized the extent to which it impacts the owner's life.

In the end, I had to come up with creative ways to manage the situation, and outside-the-box solutions. One day, not longer after we'd discovered Sierra's separation issues, C.C. was listening to me complain about how I'd wanted, just for once, a dog with no major problems. He said, "You know what this is, don't you?" I looked at him quizzically. "It's your next book!" Oh, happy day. But, as it turned out, he was right. With my new creativity and empathy firmly in place, I did end up writing *Don't Leave Me! Step-by-Step Help for Your Dog's Separation Anxiety*, which, I'm happy to report, has helped many other dogs with the same issue.

I'd be lying if I said the management part wasn't challenging. I took Sierra with me on errands, which inevitably resulted in my feeling rushed so that she wouldn't be left in the car for too long. (Interestingly, many dogs with separation anxiety do better in the car, since they know the owner normally returns quickly.) If I had an important appointment where it wasn't feasible to leave her in the car, C.C. arranged his work schedule so he could be at home with her for a few hours. I knew how lucky I was that he was willing and able to do that. Due to my writing and lecture schedule, my dog training partner was already seeing all of my training clients, which gave me one less thing to worry about. But I was still having to turn down lunches, get-togethers with friends, and other social invitations. As for C.C. and me going out together, we'd never been social butterflies, but we did enjoy movies and dining out on the weekends. Those things didn't happen for over three months. As much as I loved Sierra, I began to feel like a prisoner in my own home.

In those first few months, outside of planned separations for training purposes, I was adamant that Sierra never be left alone. It did, however, happen once. I'd woken up in the middle of the night to use the bathroom. Halfway there, I felt as though I'd been hit in the chest with a sledgehammer. Having lived with a heart condition for some time and having experienced similar pain before, I grabbed on to a door frame, tried to take smooth, calm breaths, and waited for it to pass as it normally did. But this time, not only did it not pass, but my hands went numb. *That* was new. Then I began to feel queasy. Being that I am ridiculously calm in a crisis (as long as it doesn't involve my dogs) and panic after the fact, I sat down at the computer and Googled "female heart attack symptoms." I went down the list, making mental check marks one after the other. When I reached the end, the website advised that if I had one or more of the symptoms, to kindly get off the damned computer and go call 911. So, without waking C.C., that's what I did.

After a brief explanation of why I was calling, and my hemming and hawing about whether I really should have even bothered them, the 911 operator assured me in no uncertain terms that I did need medical assistance, and instructed me to sit down and wait for the paramedics to arrive. I hung up and woke C.C.. I calmly relayed that I might have had a heart attack, and that paramedics were on the way. Poor C.C., not given to waking up bright-eyed and bushy-tailed even on the best of mornings, was more than a little confused.

It must have been a slow night, because fifteen minutes later, eight paramedics stood around me at the kitchen table. They hooked me up to monitors, asked questions, and concluded that my vital signs were stable. They tried to convince me to ride to the hospital in an ambulance but I declined, choosing to bypass the crazy-expensive transport and instead have C.C. drive me. Arriving thirty minutes later, at 4:30 a.m., we discovered that the emergency room had been closed. Permanently. Hmm. File that one under "Things that could be mentioned." So, instead of being seen in the ER, I waited a few hours to see my primary care physician.

This brilliant woman—she of the M.D. and the high salary—heard my story and opined that perhaps I had pulled a muscle. *Pulled a muscle?* Doing what? Walking from the bedroom to the bathroom? She never ordered bloodwork, which, had it been done within the proper time frame, could have offered information about the condition of my heart. Due to that oversight, I don't know to this day what really happened. What I do know is that Sierra was left by herself, locked outside in the middle of the night. I'm sure she was highly stressed. My point in sharing this story is that during this time, nothing short of a visit to the emergency room deterred me from sticking with our behavior management plan.

Not long after the heart incident, a well-known presenter on the canine lecture circuit came to town and spoke, among other things, about separation anxiety. I was already familiar with most of his philosophy, and was, for the most part, on the same page about how to handle separation issues. After the lecture, I was invited to a small dinner honoring him. By chance, I ended up sitting next to the speaker. He was a nice man, an interesting dinner companion, and, as it turned out, the owner of a dog with separation anxiety! When I told him about Sierra's issues, he couldn't understand why I was so concerned. After all, she wasn't destructive, wasn't urinating or defecating in the house, and wasn't disturbing the neighbors. So what was a little panting when I came home? As much as I liked and respected him professionally, I disagreed with this assessment. Regardless of how Sierra expressed her emotional state, she was quite clearly very distressed. And that was not all right with me.

# 7

# Sheep Herding--Baaah!

As our work continued on the separation issue, I tried to enrich Sierra's life as much as possible. She was gradually becoming more willing to engage in treat seeking, and would tentatively roll around a plastic ball with a hole in it to coax out the hidden morsels. She was also becoming a willing excavator of Kongs, so long as the way I packed them didn't make the task too difficult. We even explored puzzle-solving toys where she had to manipulate pieces by sliding or pushing at them with her paws or nose to reveal tasty tibits. She loved it all, and began to show a real enthusiasm for food. Our training sessions improved as she became less afraid and more willing to try new things. It did my heart good to see her blossom.

We often visited the local dog park in the early mornings before it got too warm and crowded. The first time we entered the enclosed area, I opened the gate and unclipped Sierra's leash. I looked down for a split second. When I looked up again, she was clear across the park. How had she gotten so far away in the blink of an eye? I still wasn't entirely sure about her breed mix, but she was apparently part rocket. She gloried in racing around the flat, open space, leaving dust clouds in her wake, scaring the pellets out of unsuspecting bunnies on the other side of the chain link fence.

Now and then we'd encounter another dog and owner. Sierra was always thrilled to see them, but knowing that many people bring aggressive or reactive dogs to the dog park, I was very careful about her play partners. For the most part, she played well with others. I say "for the most part" because she had a disconcerting way of meeting and greeting. If another dog was already in the park when we arrived, she'd shoot through the entry gate like a bullet, the hapless dog her target. Most dogs were startled by this overly enthusiastic greeting but recovered quickly, and a play session or at least mutual sniffing would follow. At other times, when Sierra was inside the park and spied a dog and owner approaching from a distance—and with her keen senses, they could be clear across the large, grassy field, at the far parking lot—she'd take a few stalking steps forward and then crouch down in the dirt and wait. When the unsuspecting dog finally walked through the gate, Sierra would spring up and run at him, and then playfully pounce. This boisterous welcome was fine with some dogs, but no doubt others didn't appreciate it. There were a few times where Sierra ran up to a dog only to suddenly put on the brakes, the thought bubble above her head reading, *Danger, Will Robinson!* Although the greetings never resulted in fights, the behavior was obviously not okay, and I couldn't let it continue.

The other problem was that Sierra was highly intolerant of other dogs trying to dominate her in any way; an attempted humping or even a paw over her back for a second too long could easily result in a fight. And although she might not *start* a fight, she would surely do her best to finish one. Dog parks aren't the safest places to begin with, so unless I knew her play partners, we began to hike the hillsides around the park perimeter instead.

I also began to brainstorm other ways to provide interesting recreation. Sierra would have made a great agility dog, but my pesky heart condition precluded me from engaging in anything that involved short bursts of running. I had no interest in competition obedience. Dock diving? Not so much a desert pursuit. Then I remembered that a friend had mentioned a woman who taught dogs sheep herding. Now, *that* might be fun! I knew nothing about herding and certainly had no experience with it, unless you count herding cockroaches out of my Brooklyn apartment's kitchen sink in the middle of the night. I wondered whether sheep herding might be something Sierra would enjoy, and hoped it could help to build her confidence. As it happened, my friend Laura had an appointment scheduled for her own dog to take a lesson the following week. She invited me along. After a quick phone call, she informed me that Judy, the instructor, had agreed to give Sierra an "instinct test" while we were there. This would gauge her natural abilities and determine whether she'd be a good candidate for herding.

As I followed Laura's truck up the narrow, winding mountain road, I wondered what Judy would make of Sierra. The stalking behavior at the park made me optimistic, since it resembled the way Border Collies move as they herd sheep. I had visions of Judy proclaiming, "She's got the instinct, alright! She's a natural if I ever saw one!" With visions of praise being heaped upon my furry honors student, the drive went quickly.

The sprawling ranch was dotted with pens filled with sheep, cattle, Border Collies, and other assorted animals. Judy was a fit and trim fifty-something woman with short, silver hair that was partially hidden under a weathered cowboy hat. Upon spying Sierra, she immediately inquired about her breed. Instead of answering the question, I asked what *she* thought Sierra looked like. Without hesitation, Judy said flatly, "She looks like a wolf." I explained that we'd just gotten Sierra's DNA test results back (out of curiosity, I had sent away for a kit), and, for what it was worth, she was allegedly a mix of Malamute, Husky, and Keeshond. I wondered whether the sheep would agree.

Like any good instructor, Judy took the time to make friends with Sierra before they began. As they stood together in a pen that contained three sheep, Judy stroked Sierra and spoke to her gently. Then Judy led her forward on leash. They walked around the pen behind the sheep, who immediately began to move away from them. The pair maintained what should have been, to the sheep, a reassuring distance. Now, I'm no expert in sheep behavior, but those sheep seemed scared. *Really* scared. Judy glanced over at me.

"Sheep tell you a lot of things about the dog," she said calmly. "These sheep are deathly afraid of her."

"Is that normal with a new dog?" I asked hopefully.

"No. It's different with every dog. But look at her. Again, she could be coyote, she could be anything. There's coyotes up here that come and sniff through the fence. So you gotta think like a sheep."

Thinking like a sheep was going to be difficult; I could barely count them to fall asleep. Still, I had to admit that Sierra might seem to them like a wild child. And who could argue with the sheep's expert opinion? In her defense, Sierra looked a bit worried about them, too. The entire time she was in the arena, when she wasn't busy nervously eyeing the sheep, her nose was on the ground, busily sniffing out every piece of poop she could find. And eating it. Perhaps this was her technique for conveying to the sheep that she was not a threat. *See? I eat your feces! I would never harm you!* The sheep remained unconvinced.

Judy kept walking Sierra around the pen, letting her get comfortable. Once she felt assured that Sierra was not going to go after the sheep, she let her off leash. She needn't have worried. Sierra kept right on scouting around for poop. That was my girl, psyching the sheep out. Probably just luring them closer...or not. After a while, I resignedly called to Judy from the sidelines.

"Umm...I guess she really doesn't have much of an instinct for this, does she?"

Judy responded kindly, "Oh, I wouldn't count her out. You're welcome to bring her back up sometime and try again. A lot of dogs are a little scared, but all of those behaviors, all that poop eating, that's because she's afraid."

Although sniffing can certainly be a stress-related behavior in dogs, and Sierra was a bit nervous, I'm pretty sure she'd eaten the poop because, to her, it was a delicacy. Besides, on hikes her nose is constantly to the ground, and anything that smells like a critter sends her into an ecstatic trance. The sheep pen might as well have had a sign hanging over it proclaiming it Doggy Disneyland.

Undeterred, Judy brought in more sheep. Maybe she figured that once their numbers had been doubled, their fear would be halved. Then she asked me to enter the pen. Now *I* was nervous. I remembered a story Laura had told me about how a bunch of sheep had pinned her to the wall. She'd been calling and calling to her dog to come and move them. Apparently, sheep aren't easily moved if you don't have four feet and a tail, and she was stuck there longer than she'd have liked. But in I went, since Judy thought it would give Sierra more confidence. Although the sheep seemed calmer than before, it became obvious that Sierra was still more interested in their excretory product than in the sheep themselves. We didn't make much progress but, on the bright side, I didn't get trampled.

Fifteen minutes later, we finally raised the white wooly flag of defeat and left the arena. A sheep in the next pen over, who had no doubt been amused by the whole debacle, pronounced very clearly, "Baaah!" I couldn't have agreed more.

*8*

# Bazooka

By the time Sierra had been with us for four months, her separation issues had improved to the point that I could leave her alone with indoor/outdoor access up to two hours. By the six-month mark, she could remain comfortably by herself for three to four hours. Although I wouldn't pronounce her "cured," she was making good progress and I was profoundly grateful to be able to return to some semblance of a normal life. Still, even with the improvements, I thought she might be happier with a canine companion. And so the search began.

Over the next few months I made some promising contacts with local mixed breed rescue groups and attended a variety of adoption events. I met plenty of adorable dogs who deserved good homes. There was Fritz, the overly enthusiastic Rottweiler mix; Simba, the Husky-Golden Retriever who resembled a giant, bouncing ball of fur; Tonka, the three-legged Malamute; and so many more. Although they each had wonderful qualities, none were the right match. I began spending an inordinate amount of time on the Petfinder and AdoptAPet websites. I've never done online dating, but I imagine it shares quite a few similarities. I entered my zip code and narrowed my search based on specific characteristics, and soon I was anxiously scrolling through photos in search of candidates who might be my type. If I found one who looked interesting, I'd read the description while keeping my fingers crossed that the personality would be as promising as the visual, or at least describe good raw material. I didn't expect perfection, and I was certainly willing to do a bit of behavior work if I had to. Hmm. Maybe it really *was* like online dating.

Some of the groups were refreshingly direct in their disclosure of the dogs' behavior issues, but others weren't quite as forthcoming. Just as saying that a person "prefers quiet dinners at home" could indicate either a romantic or someone who just can't afford a dinner out, some of the blurbs beneath the photos were a bit murky. Most legitimate rescues don't purposely try to fool anyone, but behavior problems do sometimes get downplayed in the interests of getting potential adopters to call. "Would love to be your one and only," for example, doesn't mean the dog is yearning to pledge his undying devotion; rather, if you already have a dog, forget it, as the two won't be getting along anytime soon. "Would make a great agility competitor" means you'd best be up for some serious daily exercise, or you'll find your beautiful back yard transformed into moon craters faster than you can say, "Houston, we have a problem." Then there's my perennial favorite, "In need of an experienced owner;" buckle up and hold on tight, because it's going to be a rough ride.

Like any good online dater, I narrowed my choices down to the most promising partners, and then set up meetings. And, like so many others, I discovered that's where it all falls apart. Bruno, a tall, dark and handsome Shepherd mix, was much younger than indicated. He was so wild and crazy, in fact, that I was worn out after spending a mere thirty minutes with him. Dylan the Doberman mix seemed sweet enough, but when I took him for a walk, it became clear that I would be working on his severe dog aggression issues for a long time to come. And Karma, the beautiful long-coated mixed breed, turned out not to even be the same dog I'd seen in the photo! Undaunted, I persevered. "Persevered" may be an understatement. The truth is, I became obsessed. I'd be in the midst of getting some writing done when I would suddenly feel the urge to check in on the adoption websites. After all, you never know when that perfect specimen might come along, and I wanted to be the first to check him out. I surfed the sites first thing in the morning and last thing at night, and more times in between than I care to admit. Still, the perfect match remained elusive.

September 2 was my birthday. Instead of going out to dinner, I asked C.C. if he'd go pick up a pizza from our favorite place across town. In the meantime, I scrolled through photos on Petfinder. With my mind on mouthfuls of melting cheese, I neglected to narrow the search radius to 75 miles as I normally did. I clicked on a thumbnail of a black and cream colored dog. When the photo opened to full size, all thoughts of food vanished. "It's you!" flew from my lips. I was completely sure that *this* was the dog. He was listed as a two-year-old Siberian Husky-German Shepherd mix, but he looked more like a Malamute-Shepherd mix to me. That he bore a slight resemblance to Mojo probably partly explained my instantaneous reaction, but I had come across plenty of dogs online who looked somewhat like Mojo. In fact, I'd quickly rejected those photos, not wanting to set myself up for heartache. Besides, it wouldn't give the dog a fair chance to be fully appreciated for himself. I couldn't fully explain my response to this dog, but it had been strong and certain.

In the main photo, the dog was seated. He had a long, soft-looking black and tan coat and big Shepherdy ears. His mouth was closed, his head tilted slightly, and he had a soulful, far-off look in his eyes. In another shot, he was seated but leaning slightly away from the off-camera person who was holding his leash. In the third photo, the mystery handler was attempting to pet the dog on the back. The dog's ears were in a low, worried position as he gazed straight ahead with a look that could only be described as "Get me out of here." It was good to know that my heartstrings were still fully operational, but I also knew as a trainer that the body language meant this dog wasn't entirely comfortable around people, or perhaps just not around that particular person. I wondered, *Did he have a fear of men? Was the person holding his leash a man or a woman? Could I tell from the hand? Maybe if I zoomed in a bit more…* Yep, I was in full-on Doggy Detective mode.

The dog's name was Bazooka. I hoped he'd been named him after the character in the old Bazooka Joe bubble gum comics and not after a deadly weapon, but unless the previous owner was as old as me, the chances were slim. The dog had been "surrendered by his owner after he was no longer able to afford his upkeep." Well, that wasn't uncommon, especially in a difficult economy. "Raised from a puppy, he knows his basic commands, but needs a little help in socialization." Basic commands, check. But *needs a little help in socialization…*uh-oh. I knew good and well that those words were often code for dog-aggressive, fearful, or aggressive toward people. Still, I had such a strong feeling about the dog that I was willing to learn more. Then I noticed the location: Fresno. *Fresno?* That was over 200 miles away! Oh well, what's a few hundred miles between potential family members? I remained undeterred. I did wonder how C.C. would feel about a three and a half hour drive after his stressful work week. I suspected he wouldn't be thrilled, but I also knew he'd be relieved to have an end to my incessant requests to give his opinion on yet another dog whose photo I had come across.

The next day was Friday. As soon as the shelter opened, I called and gave the clerk the impound number and asked whether she had any information other than what had been posted online. After a quick check of the records, she reported that the owner who had surrendered the dog was a college student who, as stated online, "couldn't afford his upkeep." Well, that wasn't so uncommon among kids that age. Unfortunately, that was all the information they had. I explained that we lived over three hours away and that my husband worked weekdays. I asked if she could hold on to Bazooka until we could drive up the following day. Since it was a public shelter, I knew there was a real possibility that without a hold on the dog, he might be adopted out or euthanized before we could get there. She agreed, and offered instructions for completing an online adoption application in the meantime.

At 7:00 on Saturday morning we loaded Sierra into the Jeep. The next three hours held one potty stop for Sierra, two for us, and a whole lot of speculation about the dog. Would he and Sierra get along? Would he be afraid of C.C.? Did he ride well in a car? C.C. did his best to stay awake and listen to his wife babble on about endless possibilities and potential problems. As we neared our destination, the neighborhood took on a decidedly downscale appearance. Rows of shabby houses gave way to a deserted industrial area. After a few final twists and turns, we arrived at the shelter. I asked C.C. to take Sierra for a walk around the parking lot while I went inside.

The woman at the front desk assured me that Bazooka was still there, safe and sound. I told her I'd like to meet him alone before we introduced him to Sierra. I wanted to get some idea of his personality without having another dog there to distract him. A young, perky volunteer went to fetch him. Minutes later, an underweight, scraggly black and tan dog exploded past us, dragging the girl behind him by the leash. "Bazooka! Bazooka! *Wait!*" she called, desperately trying to dig her heels in. He blazed past me and headed for the glass entry doors. I clapped my hands together a few times and called to him in a high-pitched voice. His ears pricked and he turned instantly; there was nothing wrong with his hearing, anyway. He came barreling toward me. Without slowing, he jumped up and slammed his paws roughly into my stomach. *At least he's happy to see me*, I thought gamely. He had no manners, but he also showed no aggression toward people, at least from what I could see. That was a big plus. As the volunteer caught her breath, she handed me a cookie to offer him. He snatched it from my hand, long, sharp teeth scraping skin off my palm. A shark had nothing on this boy. So, it wasn't ideal, but jumping and a hard mouth weren't huge problems. We could work on them.

I followed the volunteer into a small room with narrow wooden benches built into the walls. Bazooka seemed more interested in sniffing around the floor than in getting to know me. That was understandable, as he'd just gotten out of a shelter run and this was a new place filled with the scents of other dogs. After a few moments he approached and greeted me. He seemed to enjoy being petted, and showed no signs of minding when I handled his ears, mouth, and paws. So far so good. The bigger issue was how he would get along with Sierra. Judging from her interactions at the dog park, I guessed she would be the one to set the tone. How would she handle this pushy freight train of a boy?

I didn't want to take any chances on Bazooka attacking Sierra. Regardless of her confidence around unfamiliar dogs, he was bigger and stronger, and I didn't know how he'd react to her. I asked permission to handle him during the introductions. The volunteer seemed almost relieved as she handed the leash over. We walked Bazooka outside. When we got close to where C.C. stood with Sierra, I asked him to position himself so we could walk the dogs parallel to each other. Sierra was interested in Bazooka and wanted to approach. He didn't seem as interested, but was happy enough to walk along with all of us. After a few moments of calm walking we allowed the dogs to sniff each other's rears for a few seconds, and then walked some more. We continued that way until I was satisfied that the dogs seemed relaxed. We walked them back into the getting-to-know-you room and removed their leashes.

There was a heart-stopping moment where Sierra stood stock still, staring at the dog. I knew she was doing a lighting-fast internal assessment. I had to remind myself to breathe. Finally, after what seemed like an eternity…she play-bowed. Play-bowed! I let out a sigh of relief as Bazooka responded, if somewhat cautiously, with the proper, "Yes, let's play!" signals. Fortunately, the dogs had a very similar play style, and were soon doing joyful laps around the room, jumping excitedly on each other and communicating beautifully. C.C. and I exchanged looks of relief. He'd liked Bazooka's photo too, but had the dogs not gotten along, it would have been a deal breaker. We both knew that in the end, we weren't really the ones choosing a companion for Sierra.

We let the dogs roughhouse a bit longer, and then I interrupted the action. It's all too easy for rough play to boil over into aggression, and that was the last thing we needed. Besides, I wanted to see how Bazooka behaved around dogs other than Sierra. A little reactivity wouldn't cause me to change my mind, but I wanted to know what I was getting into. I picked up his leash and led him out into the parking lot. C.C. remained indoors with Sierra and the volunteer. We headed out across the asphalt, and soon enough we passed a Beagle being walked by another volunteer. There was no reaction from Bazooka at all, other than a curious glance. Next came a Terrier mix—again, nothing troublesome. Finally, we passed a large dog who no doubt sported a cage card declaring him "Shep X," standard shelter code for *Looks pretty Shepherdy, damned if we know what else he might be*. Although Bazooka pulled a bit toward the dog, there was no visible reactivity. Hallelujah! Back inside, I filled out the paperwork and paid the adoption fee. Ten minutes later, the new and improved Wilde pack was on the road home.

# Deadly Weapon or Enlightened Being?

*Ba-zoo-ka (noun)*
*A tube-shaped weapon, fired from the shoulder, that launches a missile that can disable a tank.*

As definitions go, it was pretty accurate. While I'm not quite a tank, by the middle of the first day with our new, rambunctious missile of a dog, I was just about disabled. I couldn't walk across a room without him grabbing a trailing hand and chomping down, or jumping up in front of me and placing his teeth around my arm, exerting a disturbing amount of pressure. This was, of course, not acceptable behavior. I'm sure some trainers would have used harsh physical corrections to quash this seemingly aggressive conduct. But besides the fact that forceful training isn't my style, and isn't ever necessary, I knew there was no aggression behind it. If anything, it was obvious that Bazooka was excited and somewhat insecure and anxious. Still, try telling that to my skin, which was covered in deep scratches that would no doubt turn to spectacular flowering purple bruises. I imagined that people would eye my arms and legs and wonder whether I needed a battered women's shelter.

I began to use my lower body as I walked to block Bazooka and drive him backward out of my personal space. I never kicked at him. Depending on where he was, sometimes it was more like shuffling forward with my feet glued to the floor, and at others, a hip bump in the way that another dog might body bump a dog who's invading his space. Bazooka might have been like a bull in a china shop, but even he started to get the message. Whenever he put his jaws around my arm, I looked at him with a hard stare, leaned my body slightly forward, and in a low voice, said, "Eh-eh." He seemed pretty fluent in Angry Mom, and backed off. I knew it would take some time for him to unlearn the bad habits he'd developed. That was okay.

Although the name Bazooka was cute in a way, I wasn't a fan of weaponry or exploding dogs. C.C. and I agreed that a change was needed. Besides, the dog didn't respond to the name anyway. To be truthful, he didn't respond to much of anything except food, which he snatched with gusto, grabbing half of the hand that was holding it for good measure. I began to ponder ideas. Something that reflected the northern part of his heritage would be appropriate. Yukon had a nice ring to it. Or maybe Tundra? I also liked Dakota. Based on his mostly-dark coat, Shadow was nice, but it was too common, as was Beau, another name I favored. Nothing seemed quite right. I loved the name D'Artagnan, but it didn't exactly flow off the tongue. I thought about it day and night. Once again, I was driving C.C. crazy over a dog. He'd be in the bathroom and I'd shout through the closed door, "What do you think about Cody?" Or, as he took out the garbage: "What about Shaman? I really like Shaman." I wondered if we shouldn't just give up and go with a name descriptive of the constant symphony of air snapping: "Clacking Jaws of Death." We couldn't come to a mutual decision. And so, for the first day, he was referred to as "The Dog Formerly Known As Bazooka" or, more prosaically, "The New Dog."

Sierra and The New Dog had been wrestling and racing in and out of the house together for what seemed like an hour, and they were finally tired. I snapped a photo of Sierra lying on her bed with The New Dog standing over her, one paw on her chest as though he were a wrestling champ hovering proudly over his pinned opponent. I had to admit that it was pretty cute. Sierra's open-mouthed grin said, *You know I'm letting you win for now, right?* I was glad to see them getting along so well. Still, I was all too familiar with the "honeymoon period" that often happens when a dog is rehomed. It's like being a guest at someone's house; the first few weeks you're on your best behavior, washing dishes and cleaning up after yourself. Then you settle in, and suddenly you're leaving potato chip crumbs all over the couch and a trail of dirty socks in your wake. Rescued dogs often don't display their true behavior issues until they've been in a home for a few weeks. Some don't even bark until they're convinced it's their home, too.

I monitored the dogs' play with hawk-like intensity and was on constant alert for any resources they might fight over. They were separated at mealtimes and when they got tasty chew bones. Even the toys got picked up when not in use. I was cautiously optimistic. The New Dog seemed to be housetrained, which was a big relief and one less thing to worry about. He might have been underweight, but at forty-eight pounds, he was still big enough to make a serious mess. The poor guy was also filthy to the point that we had to wash our hands every time we petted him. I made an appointment with the groomer for the following day.

I didn't know how The New Dog would respond to being bathed and brushed, but I figured that his being tired out before the grooming appointment could only help. So, the next morning, I rolled out of bed and into my t-shirt and sweat pants, and took the dogs to the local dog park. It was early enough that it was unlikely we'd run into other dogs. But as we crossed the field from the parking lot I could make out a large figure standing in the middle of the dog park. He was white with black patches. With his head lowered, nibbling at the grass, he was doing a wonderful impression of a grazing cow. But I knew it was Harley, a sweet male harlequin Great Dane who Sierra had played with before. The New Dog wasn't at all reactive, and even seemed mildly interested. Once inside the enclosed area, Sierra ran right up to Harley, wriggling from head to tail in greeting. Our new boy kept a slight distance but seemed comfortable. Soon Sierra was off sniffing the fascinating pee-mail left by other dogs, and the boys began to check each other out. The New Dog's body language broadcasted cautious interest, and a tentative round of gentle play ensued. Instantly, Sierra rushed the pair, forcing her body between them, effectively splitting them up. Then she turned, all teeth, and flew at our new boy. It was a lightning-fast, decisive snarling-snapping combination that drove him quickly backward, away from the Dane. Color me surprised! I knew Sierra sometimes behaved like the Dog Park Police, splitting up dogs whose play was becoming too rough, but this had seemed more like her way of saying, *That's* my *friend. Find your own playmates.* Fortunately, it was all talk and no physical damage, and the boy knew when to back off.

I too knew when to retreat, and I began to gather up the dogs' leashes so we could leave. But Harley's owner, with a forced smile on his face, called out a hasty, "Have a good day!" and beat us to it. So we stayed. I threw a tennis ball for the dogs, thinking they could channel the residual arousal and energy in a healthy way, and focus it on something other than each other. The New Dog chased the ball, and Sierra chased him. When he grabbed the ball she mugged him for it, lunging at him and snapping at his jaws. He quickly spit out the ball and looked at her in confusion as if to say, "Well, if it's *that* important to you…" What had happened to my soft, sweet girl? This was a side of her I had never seen. Maybe getting the dogs, in their elevated state of arousal, involved in a running game that could have a competitive element hadn't been the best idea. You know what they say about hindsight.

For all of their mutually enthusiastic play together at home, to say that Sierra resented the new fur-covered addition to the family would be an understatement. She'd lie on the living room rug and watch with disdain as one of us petted him. *Why would you touch that scraggly mess when you could be stroking my soft, luxuriant fur?* said the thought waves wafting our way. I couldn't blame her for being annoyed. She'd had our complete, undivided attention for the past nine months, and now this new, uncouth creature was walking all over her—literally. Whenever she would lie on her back to solicit a tummy rub, he'd immediately trot over and step on her, seeming not to notice that his foot was on her face, or paw, or wherever it happened to land. Despite Sierra's bluster at the park, at home, she never once snapped, growled, or otherwise let the young whippersnapper know that it wasn't okay to act the way he did. I wished she would.

The New Dog's lack of a concept of personal space wasn't confined to walking on Sierra. Any time I went to pet her, whether I was crouching down or just giving her a drive-by stroke down the back, he'd immediately insert his body between us and stand there demanding attention. Had no one taught this dog any manners? My immediate response was to pet each dog with one hand, straining to keep the fur-covered tank from pushing into me and knocking me over. But it was a short-term solution, and something had to be done.

While our new dog might have shown no fear when approaching Sierra, being near men was another story. He had allowed C.C. to pet him at the shelter, but at home, if C.C. was sitting on the couch and moved his foot even the tiniest bit, the dog would dart across the room, clearly afraid. This was unusual, as dogs tend to gravitate toward C.C., even if they're normally afraid of men. Had a male kicked this poor dog? I imagined a room full of drunk frat boys and thought it was entirely possible. People often ascribe a dog's fearful behavior, especially a fear of men, to having been abused, when it's often a simple lack of socialization. Dogs are naturally more afraid of men, due to their larger size, deeper voices, and, well, the testosterone. But in this case I thought there really might have been a history of physical abuse.

In the meantime, I wanted to begin some real training with The New Dog, and for that, I needed to be able to address him by name. I couldn't very well call him to me by yelling, "Dog Who Was Formerly Known As Bazooka! Come!" Given his rambunctious jumping and mouthing, his pushiness, and his general lack of a clue as to how to behave, I wondered whether a more peaceful, intelligent name might influence things for the better. Peace? A great name, but it didn't exactly fit him. Ditto for Harmony. In the end, we decided on Bodhi, short for Bodhisattva.

*Bo-dhi-satt-va (noun)*
*One whose essence is enlightenment; an enlightened, compassionate being.*

It was a vast improvement over a deadly weapon, anyway, and something to aspire to. An enlightened being. One could only hope.

*Soko's beauty shot. What she was looking at? Yep, the ball.*

*Soko with Mojo the Tank Puppy.*

*Me and
my soul dog
Mojo.*

*Did I mention
that Mojo was
taller and longer
than most dogs?*

*Sierra, a.k.a. Mommy's Little Predator.*

*Bodhi and Sierra at play. It's rare to catch Sierra looking this goofy!*

*Though it might not look like it, this too is play!*

*Could you stay mad at that face?*

*Practicing to be in KISS.*

*Bodhi: From bad boy to cover boy!*

*Here comes my girl--and her crazy tail.*

*You've gotta love models who will work for hot dogs.*

*The sky was so pretty one morning before we headed to the park that I couldn't resist posing Bodhi and Sierra on the hillside.*

*10*

# Day Ten

On our tenth day with Bodhi, the fighting began. The dogs had been wrestling in the foyer, growling and carrying on in a commendable display of northern breed rough and tumble play. They leaped on each other's backs. They grabbed mouthfuls of fur. Suddenly, the vocalizations changed from good-natured competition to something more ominous. Play was boiling over into aggression. Some believe it's best to let unfamiliar dogs "work things out," but there's a difference between allowing squabbles to be settled, and seeing a potential bloodbath in the making. Besides, Bodhi had ten pounds or so on Sierra, and I wasn't about to see her hurt. I stepped in and calmly separated the two, silently giving thanks that neither redirected and bit me. Things settled down within a few seconds. That, at least, was a good sign.

The play skirmishes concerned me, but at least they only seemed to happen in my presence. When the dogs were outside running around on their own everything was fine, so I wasn't worried about keeping them separated when we were gone. Sometimes when fights happen only in an owner's presence, it's because one of the dogs views the owner as a valuable resource to guard. That seemed to be the case with us, given what happened soon after.

The following morning, I had locked the dogs outside and left to do errands. An hour later I returned and opened the dog door to let them inside. Sierra and Bodhi were all sparkling eyes, wagging tails, and adorable pet-me looks. I crouched down and began to pet them both. Suddenly, the happy wags and angling for position turned into a flurry of snapping jaws. They were snarling at each other, and I was caught in the middle. I quickly stood up and, as calmly as possible, got them under control. There was no physical damage to any of us, but the jealousy between them was not a good thing. I hoped things would settle down over the coming weeks.

There was another problem with Bodhi, though. Saying he was destructive would be like saying the Titanic had a bit of a leak. One morning, I'd awakened to find that he'd torn most of the carpeting off the outdoor dog ramp that had originally been built for Mojo. He had also grabbed a few towels that had been sitting on top of the washing machine, taken them outside, and torn them to bits. At other times, he shredded a book I'd left lying on the living room coffee table (ironic, since my daytime stress-relief breaks had consisted of lying on the couch and reading), a pair of reading glasses (do I detect a theme?), a blanket, and a television remote control. He would also grab things off shelves or other low areas that, to make them inaccessible, would have meant completely rearranging our living space; in our foyer alone, the wall-to-wall bookcases were filled with CDs, DVDs, and photos in frames. There were also small stand-alone bookcases that held what a friend would call *chachkas*...little wolf statues and other trinkets. It was hard to predict what Bodhi would destroy next.

So why, you might wonder, hadn't he been crated overnight? Because when we had tried it the first night, we'd discovered he was leaking urine. A veterinary visit was in his near future, but for now, we couldn't very well let him lie in a puddle and end up with urine scald or worse. We also couldn't lock him outside because, as we soon discovered, he would bark and howl in a non-stop anxiety meltdown. Our neighbors aren't all that far away, and waiting it out wasn't an option. I also didn't want to have to get out of bed at 2 a.m. to yell at him to be quiet. Gating him off indoors didn't work because he'd simply destroy anything within the gated area. And we didn't dare tether him to a piece of furniture for fear that he would eat it.

It would have been bad enough if the destruction only took place overnight, but it was likely to happen any time I left the room or even looked away for more than two seconds. It was unbelievable! I reflected on the irony of having refused to get a puppy, who surely would have been less of a handful. Now I was stuck with an adolescent who you would think had been raised by wolves—only wolves have better manners.

Normally, if a dog of mine grabs something he shouldn't, I utter a sharp, "Eh-eh!" until I can teach the more instructive "Leave It," meaning "Step away from the object." But whenever I'd raise my voice to Bodhi, Sierra's ears would flatten and she'd make that "Please don't beat me" face. That made things challenging. I tried clapping my hands instead to interrupt Bodhi, but even that scared Sierra. I finally ended up stalking over to Bodhi and putting my face up to his, saying, "No" in a low, growly voice while making the most scowly, unpleasant face I could muster. It worked, except for every now and then when he would look at me blankly as if to say, *What's with you? Did you just eat a lemon? And is there any left for me?* Non-compliance earned him a time out outside, which he hated.

Sierra, at least, was earning her keep. One day, I'd been working at the computer when I heard a tiny, high-pitched "Eeep!" I froze in place and listened. Silence. I waited. The next time it happened, I stood up and tried to determine where the sound had originated. Within a few repetitions, I realized it was coming from the closet where I kept office supplies. This was clearly a job for Super Prey Drive Girl! I called Sierra in and motioned toward the closet. She immediately sprung into action, stealthily inspecting the area as I pulled cardboard shipping boxes and manila envelopes out of her way. Suddenly, she froze. Seconds later, she emerged with a tiny, grey, furry body in her mouth. Although it's hard to say "Good girl!" when what you really want to say is "Ewwww!" I praised her and enthusiastically encouraged her to take the mouse outside. She did, and, after a few seconds, returned and repeated the maneuver. Soon the tally was five baby mice. *Why is my closet suddenly the Mickey Mouse Club?* I wondered. Maybe there was a tiny disco ball, miniscule leather couches and cheese trays in there. I wondered if *Muskrat Love* was playing. For the moment, at least, Sierra seemed satisfied that the mice were gone.

Unfortunately, not everything was so promising. Every morning, I'd wake up to see what Bodhi had destroyed. Sure, I could have locked him outside overnight and dealt with the barking by using some device that would scare him into being quiet. But for all his bluster, he seemed so fragile, so insecure and anxious, that I didn't want to cause him any further distress. And so I chose to chance physical damage to our belongings over emotional damage to the dog.

I couldn't help missing those quiet mornings when I would rise to find Sierra lying peacefully on the living room couch, awaiting our long, luxuriant petting sessions. I remembered the peaceful walks we'd taken at the park, and relaxing on the floor with her at home without worrying about a big bruiser of a dog stepping on us. Although I understood all too well that we'd adopted an adolescent dog who had no training or manners, I longed for our previously peaceful household. I worried about the fighting, the destruction, and so many other things that I wondered if I had it in me to work through all of Bodhi's issues. I kept thinking, *I'm too old for this s#(%!* It hadn't been more than two weeks since we'd brought Bodhi home, and I was already wondering if it had been a mistake. But it was early, and I owed it to him to try.

11

# The Honeymoon's Over

The problem of Bodhi morphing into an attention-demanding torpedo whenever I petted Sierra had to be solved. It was rude, it annoyed Sierra, and it irritated me, too. I needed to teach Bodhi that me giving Sierra attention was a very good thing. I tethered him to the living room table and, as he lay there on his dog bed, fed him treats as I petted her. *See? My petting her means good things for you.* He seemed content enough to lie there and accept treats, and didn't even attempt to get up. So far, so good. After a few days of practice sessions, I switched tactics. My goal was that eventually, whenever I went to pet Sierra, Bodhi would take that as a cue to lie down and wait to be petted. It sounded good on paper, but it was harder to teach than I expected. Oh, Bodhi was a smart enough— he'd learned quickly to lie down and stay on cue—but intelligence is a lot different than impulse control. He possessed a good amount of the former but almost none of the latter. So we kept at it, practicing a little bit each day.

Meanwhile, the destruction continued. We tried to keep counters and tabletops clear, but there would inevitably be times where one of us laid something down and walked away for a moment. One day I walked out of my office to find that C.C. had put the day's mail on the kitchen table. There was a refund check from the IRS—well, it *used* to be a refund check. Now it was a sad-looking pile of shredded paper with a piece of envelope sporting the IRS logo. Imagine what fun it was to explain to the IRS representative that my dog had eaten my refund check. I was starting to understand all too well how the kid who had surrendered Bodhi to the shelter "couldn't afford his upkeep." On the plus side, Bodhi hadn't behaved badly at the groomer's, and he now looked like an adorable stuffed animal. My response whenever he did something that irked me became, "It's a good thing you're cute!"

Bodhi's behavioral issues were a constant challenge, but there was something troubling me even more. He was the first dog I'd ever had where we just weren't bonding. It usually takes me half a second to fall in love with a dog and, true to form, it had been instantaneous with Sierra. Sure, I'd had an immediate feeling of connection upon seeing Bodhi's photo, but I just wasn't feeling it in person. The situation was completely alien, and it worried me. But, I reasoned, not feeling warm and fuzzy toward a being who's turned your peaceful life upside down was certainly understandable.

While I might not have been head over heels about Bodhi, I was determined to take as good care of him as possible. In addition to his behavior problems, he still had the physical one—the urine leak. I had made an appointment with our veterinarian, but in the meantime, I did some research on the internet. Here's what I learned: online self-diagnosis is never the best idea, whether looking up symptoms for a person or a dog. It only served to scare me that Bodhi might have some horrible disease. I tried not to think about it. Besides, I had other things to worry about—the resource guarding issues had gotten worse.

The dogs had taken to getting into skirmishes over anything they perceived as valuable, and as far as I could tell, Bodhi was the one who always started it. I had been extremely careful. At the time, I was feeding a high quality dry kibble, which I placed into plastic balls they could roll around until the pieces fell out. For meals, Bodhi was gated in the kitchen. The dog door was just off the kitchen, so he had access if he needed to urinate. Sierra, who had the foyer to herself, would expertly paw at her ball, coaxing the treats out smoothly, one after another. She'd steal pitying glances at Bodhi, who was awkwardly trying to bat the ball around or crush it in his jaws. *Boy, have you got a lot to learn*, her disdainful looks conveyed. But the arrangement worked. I continued to separate them whenever they got treats or chew items. But one afternoon as I rinsed out an empty Kong in the sink, Bodhi lunged at Sierra just behind my knees. Snarling erupted, and I had to separate them. Bodhi had actually been guarding the Kong from a distance, even though it was empty.

The constant vigilance required to prevent Bodhi from destroying things, to keep the dogs from fighting, and to clean up Bodhi's urinary drippings was exhausting. It was difficult for me to get any work done, and even more difficult to maintain a positive attitude. I wasn't sleeping well, and I felt myself becoming increasingly cranky. Poor C.C. would come home from work each night to a litany of complaints, and although he listened patiently, I'm sure he would have much preferred to be having a beer and reading the newspaper in peace. I didn't like the constant stream of negativity flowing from my mouth either, but I couldn't seem to help it.

Early mornings before C.C. went to work were the best times for all of us. He'd take one dog out for exercise, and I'd take the other. Because it was wintertime when the rattlesnakes were on vacation, C.C. was able to hike in the mountains behind our house. He'd use a long line, which allowed for running, jumping, and even chasing of critters as he ran behind. Both dogs had amazing stamina and a relentless enthusiasm for exploring. They soon whipped C.C. into better shape than he'd been in for years. While he was hiking with one dog, I'd take the other to the park or for a long walk, and we would work on training skills. We switched off daily. It was a good arrangement. I'd come home to hear from C.C. how Sierra, despite being on a long line, had chased a bunny, or how she'd spied a coyote in the distance; or, he would tell me how Bodhi had leaped, gazelle-like, over a small stream. In turn, I'd proudly relate how Bodhi had maintained a sit-stay at the park in the face of distractions, or how Sierra had delighted in finding a new playmate.

On one of our first days at the park, I'd introduced Bodhi to Niko, a calm, handsome six-year-old male Husky who belonged to my friend Kathy. Bodhi had cautiously approached Niko and sniffed him. Niko didn't seem especially interested, but allowed it. We walked the dogs together for a while, with Bodhi following Niko around, sniffing wherever Niko sniffed. Maybe he figured Niko knew something he didn't. Back at the parking lot, Bodhi play bowed. Niko didn't respond. He seemed almost amused by Bodhi, regarding him as though he were a youngster who needed direction and manners. He was perceptive, that Niko. That the dogs got along was a relief, as I enjoyed my morning walks with Kathy. But even though Bodhi was fine with Niko—perhaps because we'd introduced them so early on—he had begun to lunge and bark at other dogs we passed. There was something about being on leash around other dogs that caused him to be reactive. It was a textbook case of leash frustration. And so we had one more thing to add to the list of challenges.

At least I didn't have to worry as much when I left Sierra at home now, since she was no longer alone. It was unfortunate that she had to be locked out of the house along with Bodhi because of his appetite for destruction, but they seemed content enough outdoors. I would come home to find both dogs lying on the ramp or lazily wrestling, and remind myself how much better it was for Sierra to have a companion. When the two played nicely, they both obviously enjoyed it. And their play styles were strikingly similar. One would wrap a paw over the other's shoulders, or jump from the side in an attempt at a takedown. They'd spin and dart to and fro, and then race around like fur-covered maniacs. It was fun to watch, and gave me hope that they would eventually get along more of the time.

There were periods when I'd have a few minutes or even a few hours where I felt more optimistic about Bodhi—and then something else would happen. Two weeks after we brought him home, I was taking a much-needed break from the book I was writing about separation anxiety. I was lying on the living room couch reading, with a box of peanut butter crackers wedged between my body and the back of the couch. Sierra came walking up through the narrow corridor formed by the couch and the coffee table. She sniffed the air and then the couch. I patiently explained that although peanut butter was indeed one of the world's finest inventions, the crackers weren't for her. Just then Bodhi approached from the opposite direction. Now the dogs were nose to nose in a very small space, with me in the middle. Before you could say "Not good," a snarkfest broke out. Jaws clacked and snarls filled the air as the dogs lunged at each other. I wedged the book between them (now, there's one advantage of a solid book over a Kindle) and simultaneously sprang up, employing reflexes I didn't know I still possessed. Sierra seemed scared, while Bodhi just looked puzzled. I calmed the dogs down, put the crackers away, and made a mental note that the Fear of Clacking Jaws Diet could be quite the effective deterrent against late afternoon couch snacking.

Bodhi, still worked up after all the excitement, began to race around looking for things to shred, grabbing at my hands and arms in the process. I'd had it. I told him, "Too bad," put him outside, and closed the dog door. Exhausted and frazzled, I put my head in my hands and tried to calm down. What had happened to my life? If there was an "undo" button that could reverse our having adopted Bodhi, at the moment, I felt sure I would press it. I hadn't wanted a project, and this was clearly going to be, if not a life-long project, one that could take years. It wasn't just a matter of having to train a dog who was misbehaving or lacked socialization. Those issues were understandable, especially with an adolescent. The thing that concerned me more, other than the relationship between the dogs and my not bonding with Bodhi, was something I couldn't quite put my finger on. I felt there was something about the way Bodhi was *wired* that was just…off. He reminded me of people I had been around who were constantly jittery, unfocused, and seemed uncomfortable in their own skin. It was as though he was perpetually anxious and strangely unfocused. And he was *jumpy*. Aa spoon dropping on the kitchen floor would send him flying. His nervous energy was constantly turned up to 11 on a dial that should have only gone to 10. Although he seemed to be warming up to C.C. somewhat, he was still nervous around him. Even when I petted him, his eyes never got that soft, half-lidded look that most dogs get when they're enjoying human contact. I wondered if he really was a "special needs" kind of dog, and how much anything I did would help.

I had mentioned to C.C. early on that I thought we'd made a mistake. I know, it sounds awful. As someone who's worked in rescue, I'm the first to say that dogs are not sweaters, to be exchanged when they don't fit in the way you expected. But when you've got years of experience with dogs and behavior, you know all too well what a massive project looks like. If this was how Bodhi acted during the initial period when most dogs are on their best behavior—the "honeymoon period," as rescuers call it—how much worse would it be in the months and years to come? *Would* he eventually injure Sierra? That would be a deal breaker. The view down the road was not pretty, and it was a trip I didn't want to make. We hadn't had Bodhi very long, and I told myself there was nothing wrong with finding him another home. It was as though he'd had a brief vacation—a doggie Club Med where the guests were fed, well cared for, and allowed to trash their rooms. Rehoming was something to keep in mind, although I felt guilty at even entertaining the thought. And, I'd only be passing the problem on to the next person, and that might not end well for Bodhi.

It didn't help that my conscience—that annoying voice that offered wisdom like, *You've got a writing deadline* and *Do you really need that piece of chocolate cake?*—constantly chided: *You're a professional trainer. You've written books. You teach seminars to other trainers, for crying out loud! You should be able to fix this.* That might be true, I argued, but I shouldn't *have* to take on this type of hardship for who knew how long, possibly causing harm to Sierra in the process. I would be affecting *all* of us with this decision, and I felt a huge responsibility to make the right one. I would have slept on it, had I been able to forego the constant whirring of worry and get a decent night of uninterrupted sleep.

# The Peanut Butter Couch Skirmish
# Part Deux

I've had back problems for years. They had started back in the Mojo and Soko days, when both were seniors and beginning to weaken physically from age and degenerative myelopathy. Plus, Mojo had torn a cruciate ligament. Recovery was a slow process, to say the least. Both dogs could walk but neither could stand up from a lying or sitting position without help. I ended up lifting each of them at least twenty times a day, sometimes with the assistance of a sling and sometimes without, depending on the situation. With Soko weighing in at ninety pounds and Mojo at 120, my back quickly gave out. I never recovered. My life became a series of visits to doctors and chiropractors, and I dealt with the pain as best I could. One thing I'd learned over the years was that emotional stress caused my back muscles to tense up and sometimes spasm, which would make the pain excruciating. With all of the tension surrounding the situation with Bodhi and Sierra, I was in pain the majority of my waking hours. That, in turn, made being patient and compassionate all the more challenging.

The day after the Peanut Butter Couch Skirmish was a Saturday. I was lying on the couch in the early evening with an ice pack on my lower back. There wasn't a speck of cracker or other food in the vicinity. C.C. was relaxing on the other couch watching television. As the newscaster droned on, I drifted off to sleep. Suddenly, I was jolted awake by very loud, extremely close snarls and clacking teeth. My eyes flew open. The dogs were snapping at each other—directly in front of my face! I struggled upright and stood as quickly as I could while separating them. It had all happened so fast.

I got the dogs calmed down, took a deep breath, and asked C.C. if he'd seen what had happened. He said Sierra had walked over to lick me on the face. Bodhi had apparently taken offense to this and rushed her, which had started the fight. I hadn't expected there to be a problem without food present, or when I wasn't actively petting them. I had been hyper-vigilant about their interactions and management regarding anything that could be construed as a valuable resource. While it was nice to be considered a valued resource myself, how could I manage anything while unconscious? This was too much. I knew adopted dogs could come with issues, of course, but these dogs seemed to have brought along enough baggage to fill the belly of a plane.

As much as the unexpected skirmishes left me feeling frustrated and upset, I did have control in one area—training. I had been diligently practicing with each dog separately as well as working with them both together. On cue, Bodhi and Sierra could now Sit, Down, Stay, and Come in tandem. Both also had the beginnings of a solid "Leave It." We regularly practiced impulse control exercises as well, such as sitting and waiting to be released to eat or to walk through a doorway.

A bright spot throughout the entire ordeal was my email correspondence with a good friend. Valerie had three Pugs and a German Shepherd, and also happened to be an excellent professional dog trainer. The Shepherd had been her special dog, and he'd recently passed away. She hadn't planned on getting another dog anytime soon, but when a friend's German Shepherd had a litter, she fell in love with one of the puppies and couldn't resist. As it turned out, Dexter wasn't what you'd call an easy puppy. Even as an experienced trainer, Valerie wondered what she had gotten herself into. We quickly became a two-person support group. I would email Val at 4:00 a.m. wondering how I could possibly make this work with Bodhi. I'd confess my fantasies of finding a rescue group who might take him. The next day I would find a return email filled with compassion, support, and useful ideas. I tried my best to do the same for her. It's a strange phenomenon that even experienced trainers can have blind spots when the dog in question is their own. Personal involvement has a way of turning problems that would normally be solvable, or at least manageable, into a fuzzy haze of emotional confusion.

The next day I took Bodhi to see the veterinarian. Fortunately, there were no other dogs in the waiting room. Once in the exam room the vet, a kind, gentle woman, patiently tried to coax a very nervous Bodhi to her.

Even offering the yummy treats I had surreptitiously slipped her didn't convince him. Finally, between the two of us, we got him restrained so she could listen to his heart. (I thought he'd be more comfortable with me restraining him than the vet tech, and fortunately, they allowed it.) She then led Bodhi on leash to the back of the clinic for a blood draw and urine tests. When she returned, she mentioned that Bodhi had been none too happy about the restraint. I asked her to show me which holds they used, so I could practice them at home.

As far as his urine issues, we'd know more in a few days. One thing the vet *could* tell me right away was that she didn't believe Bodhi was two years old. By the looks of his teeth, he was probably more like a year to a year-and-a-half. C.C. and I had suspected as much, as he most definitely behaved like an adolescent. Of course, being younger also meant he was more likely to be the rambunctious, crazed frat boy he was for that much longer. Oh, joy!

# 13

# Got Any Pizza or Beer?

By the following week, the buildup of stress and lack of sleep had completely unraveled me. That might explain why, with my debilitated brain function, I ended up leaving the dogs loose in the house while I went out to do errands. After visiting the post office and the supermarket, I returned to find that Bodhi had eaten a telephone receiver. Perhaps he had tried to call out for pizza. We'd only had two phones to begin with, and this one's base had been installed near the living room so we wouldn't have to rush across the house to answer the kitchen phone. I was going to have to get my lazy butt off the couch from now on, because the object that used to be a telephone was lying out back, the battery compartment torn out, exposed wires waving every which way. Bodhi had also somehow pried the metal lid off the poop can. There, strewn across the entire back of the house, was a scene you might find in a dictionary under "shit storm." It was an appropriate metaphor for the entire situation, if you asked me. A few towels had been dragged outside for good measure, as well as a pillow from the couch, although for some reason he hadn't torn up the pillow. Perhaps he'd been Dog Interrupted.

In the meantime, Bodhi was still leaking urine, so crating him was impossible. His medical tests had come back clean, so the cause of the leakage was still a mystery. Crating wouldn't have completely solved the problem anyway, as the destruction wasn't limited to when he was left alone in the house. Sometimes I didn't even have to be out of the room for Hurricane Bodhi to strike. One day I was sitting at the computer in my office trying to focus on work when he walked in and calmly began to chew on a power cable beneath the desk. *Really?* It was non-stop.

I found myself thinking of an experience we'd had before Bodhi had come along. Early on, we had taken Sierra on a trip to Big Bear, where we'd rented a small cabin in the woods. There was no television, no internet, and very little contact with the outside world. It was lovely. We got up in the mornings and hiked the woods together, with Sierra on a long line, tracking and sniffing out every squirrel, mouse, and other critter within range. She was in heaven. We were, too. We talked and laughed as she explored, and took photos of her posed on fallen logs and against beautiful backdrops of trees and flowers. There was a small town with shops and restaurants nearby, and some of the eateries allowed dogs on the patio. C.C. couldn't envision Sierra lying there calmly as we ate. I couldn't blame him. He was probably remembering Mojo, who, although he would have behaved, never would have been truly relaxed with other dogs around in such a close space. But I took along a stuffed Kong and a heaping serving of optimism, and off we went. Entering the restaurant's charming stone patio, I scanned the area and chose a table in the back corner so that entering dogs wouldn't have to pass us, and we'd be out of the way of foot traffic. I gave Sierra the Kong, we ordered our food, and soon we were having one of those nice, relaxing days that didn't seem noteworthy at the time, but upon reflection, would be recalled with fondness and longing for years to come.

A firm believer in things happening for a reason, I wondered what the bigger rationale might be when it came to Bodhi. He was here because of my own actions, of course. But was there something below the surface as well, some lesson I was supposed to learn? Surely I could stand to develop more patience in life, and this experience was certainly the perfect vehicle. I resolved to try harder to stop looking back at what we'd lost in our special solo relationship with Sierra, and to do everything in my power to make things work out with Bodhi.

I realized that a lot of the destruction happened on weekday mornings while C.C. was eating breakfast and reading the newspaper and I was still asleep. C.C. is not what you'd call a morning person, and keeping an eye on the dogs when he was still semi-conscious was not going to happen. So I asked him to put the dogs outside and close the dog door as soon as he got up. They could play and amuse themselves out back until I was awake to watch them. I began crate training Bodhi a little bit at a time, so that once the urinary issue was cleared up, he could be confined for short periods when necessary. I fed some meals in the crate too, and he was soon able to chew calmly on his bully sticks with the crate door closed.

Strangely, the tide seemed to be turning as far as his relationship with Sierra. Where I'd been concerned that he might hurt her, now she was beginning to get snarky with him. One day, an hour after they'd been fed, the two were wrestling on the foyer carpet I had dubbed The Wrestling Mat. Sierra had perfected maneuvers such as the Grab and Spin, where she clenched Bodhi's collar in her teeth and spun him around as he lay on the carpet. He didn't seem to mind. The balance of power during play had been going back and forth, as it often did. But suddenly things went from a friendly romp to a serious discussion about who was in charge. At some point Sierra clearly said, "That's alpha bitch to you!" After a flash of teeth and a brief skirmish, Bodhi seemed convinced. He backed off.

The next morning, I awoke to find that C.C. had, as requested, put both dogs out back as soon as he awoke. He'd had his breakfast, read his paper, and gone off to work. Half asleep, I shambled toward the kitchen window to peer out back. I expected to find the dogs napping, having run around and played all morning. What I found instead was something my mind couldn't quite make sense of at first. When the mental fog cleared, I realized I was looking at the remains of the mini-fridge that had been standing next to the meat freezer. The fridge hadn't held any food or bones for quite some time, but who knows, maybe the frat boy thought there was some beer in there. The bungee cable that had been wound around the fridge for extra security had been chewed through. The entire fridge was lying on its side with the door wide open, hanging by a hinge. The plastic shelves had been demolished, and the insulation had been torn out and chewed up. It was a mess. Sierra looked extremely worried, as though she knew there would be yelling. Whoever had her before we did had certainly ingrained a fear of being reprimanded. Bodhi just wagged his tail and looked at me, Bart Simpson but with even less of a clue. How long could this go on?

*14*

# Thanksgiving Stuffing

Bodhi's reactivity toward other dogs while on leash was another thing we needed to address. We would pass another dog and he'd growl low in his throat or, depending on the dog, lunge while releasing a mad flurry of barks. Because really, when you have a dog who destroys everything in sight, has anxiety issues, is pushy, fights with your other dog, and leaks urine everywhere, what you really need is for him is to also be reactive with other dogs. Well, there was nothing to do but work on it. In the early mornings while C.C. hiked with Sierra, I worked with Bodhi at the park. Of course, we had already practiced quite a bit at home first. I didn't expect him to be able to pay attention to me around distractions without ever having taught him what I wanted first in a quiet environment where he could learn and succeed. Day after day we walked around the park, keeping a safe distance from other dogs, and soon Bodhi began to get the idea that not only was it rewarding to pay attention to me instead of them, but that there was something else he could do when he felt uncomfortable, other than lunging and barking. The hot dog pieces definitely helped. Things were going well.

The next week I was working at the computer as usual, having locked the dogs outside. When I let them back in, Sierra had something in her mouth. Cringing in dread that it might be something soft and furry, I parted her jaws and reached inside to remove the object. It was a piece of particle board. Confused, I looked around. Where had *that* come from? I glanced out the back door to find that Bodhi had not only torn strips of carpeting off the dog ramp, but he'd apparently been chewing up the particle board that formed the foundation of the nearest storage shed. I took a deep breath. Let's see... I still couldn't crate him because of the urinary issue. I couldn't leave him outside without risking major destruction, despite the fact that he was getting plenty of exercise and should have been tired.

He'd had bloodwork to rule out any medical reasons for his behavior. The boy just couldn't seem to relax and chill out. I thought about various behavioral protocols or alternative therapies that might help, but I was stretched so thin physically, mentally, and emotionally that I couldn't muster up the energy to think it through clearly.

Regardless of my state of mind, one thing needed immediate attention: Bodhi's handling issues. Like many dogs, he didn't like being touched in certain ways, especially around the paws. He conveyed this aversion by placing his mouth around my hand and applying gentle pressure while looking at me as if to say, *Please don't make me bite down harder.* While he was entitled to his preferences, there were foxtails growing on our property that blew everywhere and could be dangerous and even fatal if they worked their way into a dog's mouth, ears, nose, or body. The pointy, dried weeds tended to lodge between furry toes, and I knew I was going to have to check Bodhi's paws regularly during the summer months. Besides, when I'd had the mobile groomer out to bathe the dogs, they'd mentioned that Bodhi had seemed very uncomfortable with being handled. And so, I began doing exercises that involved Bodhi being rewarded with treats for lying calmly and allowing me to handle him. It soon became clear, though, that food—even a low-value, dry cookie—was too motivating; I guess it's difficult to lie calmly when you're levitating. So instead, I went about it slowly and patiently, stroking and calming him, then taking a brief peek between the toes. More petting, then another peek. I was soon able to remove four or five foxtails during a session with Bodhi putting his mouth on my hand only once. It was progress.

~ * ~ * ~ * ~ * ~ * ~ * ~ * ~ * ~ * ~ * ~ * ~ *

As September's heat gave way to the falling leaves of October, there were other improvements. Bodhi was starting to get the idea that in order to get attention at home he would have to stop inserting himself between Sierra and me. He would, as we'd practiced, lie down nearby instead. The behavior wasn't quite solid yet, but he was doing it more of the time, and that was good enough for now. For his reactivity toward other dogs, I had begun to use a head halter, which Bodhi did not love wearing, but things were progressing to the point that when he saw another dog, rather than lunging and barking, he would look to me automatically for treats and praise.

I was in the process of completing my book on separation anxiety, and although I often worked from sunup to sundown (I'm self-employed, but my boss is a slave-driver), it felt good to know that the information would help others whose dogs were suffering. October soon turned to November, and our closest friends invited us over for Thanksgiving dinner. Years ago when C.C. and I played in a band together, Jerry had been our guitarist. His wife Laura and I had become good friends. I was glad for the dinner invitation, not only because my culinary skills are non-existent, but for the much-needed opportunity to spend time with friends and just relax.

But where to leave the dogs while we were gone? Over time, I'd discovered that Bodhi was calmer when left with indoor-outdoor access. Like many dogs, he had a sort of barrier frustration. If he was locked outside he wanted in, and vice versa. That, in turn, created stress, which resulted in destruction and other unwanted behaviors. I had gradually begun to leave the dogs free in the house with the dog door open and, over time, Bodhi's destructive habits had lessened somewhat. But his grab-it-and-go tendencies weren't completely gone. Because his standard mode of operation was to snatch things off the washing machine and countertops and drag them outside, my strategy of late had been to clear all decks but to leave a "legal" object where he could just reach it. I would line up four empty Kongs, some out of reach, others where he could grab them. It had worked well. I'd be gone and Bodhi would grab one of the Kongs, take it outside, and chew on it. I couldn't have actually stuffed the Kongs for fear the dogs would fight over them; but with the empty Kongs there was no fighting, and Bodhi's need to pillage seemed to be satisfied. Jerry and Laura lived nearby, and we expected to be gone for three or four hours at the most. The dogs' "alone time" had been gradually built up to three and a half hours, so I wasn't too worried about their stress levels. With promises of bringing home tasty leftovers, we took our leave.

As we entered our friends' home, we were surrounded by the tantalizing aroma of sinfully rich desserts baking. Dinner was served later than expected, but it was so wonderful to chat with friends and meet new people that I just didn't care. Finally, we all enjoyed a wonderful meal. After dinner there was wine, and although I could have happily stayed all night socializing, I began to be concerned about the dogs. I'd be talking and laughing, and suddenly the dogs would pop into my mind. After it had happened a few times, I became convinced that it was more than normal worry, and was, in fact, one of those intuitive feelings that shouldn't be ignored. I told C.C. we needed to leave. During the drive home, I realized we'd been gone for almost five hours. The sky was already dark and, although the dogs had indoor access, they had never been left alone during the evening hours.

As we opened the front door, I noticed some white fluff in the entryway. *Oh, crap. Did Bodhi get hold of a pillow?* I thought. As we walked in, my thoughts changed to, *That's an awful lot of stuffing for a pillow.* I followed the trail into the living room. There was our beautiful Southwestern couch—the one we'd been amazingly lucky enough to find, the one that perfectly matched our other couch, the one I really, really liked—torn to bits. The fabric that served as a backrest had been slashed horizontally all the way across, the entire panel disemboweled. Something inside me snapped. I suddenly found myself with one hand around Bodhi's collar, the other waving a wad of stuffing in his face as I shouted out my anger and frustration. I was *pissed.* Granted, it wasn't my most shining moment. (Later, when I related the story to my mother, she said, "I thought you weren't supposed to reprimand them after the fact?" I knew I shouldn't have let her read my books.) It was partly my own fault, as I could have erred on the side of caution and locked the dogs outside. C.C., strangely, didn't seem quite as angry. Or maybe he was just being rational, and realized there wasn't much we could do about now. I cleaned up the mess, unable to even look at Bodhi. I hated living like this, seeing things I cared about destroyed, feeling constantly exhausted, stressed out, and trapped. It felt like each time we would take two steps forward, we went flying five steps back.

# The Cuddle Offensive

Although the couch incident was a low point, we were making steady progress in other areas. Bodhi's reactivity toward his fellow canines was improving, so long as the other dog didn't invade his space or begin to bark. Week after week, we practiced together around the local parks and mountain trails. One morning, C.C. took Bodhi for a walk while I had Sierra at Niko the Husky's house for a play date. C.C. normally avoids other dogs when walking one of ours, but on this day, a woman walking a small dog appeared unexpectedly from around a corner, and… nothing! Bodhi did great. There was no growling and no lunging. Hurray for classical conditioning! It looked like all of our practice was starting to pay off.

Sadly, the lack of feeling bonded with Bodhi hadn't improved. But I still felt the responsibility to resolve his behavior problems. The underlying cause of most of it seemed to stem from his deep-seated insecurity and anxiety. Who knew how much was attributable to his early life, and how much might be genetic? Either way, I wondered if my lack of feelings of attachment was making it worse. There was no way around the fact that I didn't pay as much attention to him or give him as much affection as I did Sierra. Sure, I made it a point to pet him when I did her, but dogs have good instincts, and I'm betting he could feel the difference. But what could I do? There was nothing written on the subject, at least nothing I could find. I thought long and hard about it.

Finally, I did something that might sound odd: I mounted a Cuddle Offensive. Whenever Bodhi was lying quietly (or was at least not in full levitation mode), I cuddled and petted him, and offered calm affection. He received long strokes down his silky fur, coupled with the squinted eyes and gently smiling mouth that I would naturally use for Sierra. It's not as though I was totally faking it. No doubt I felt some true affection for Bodhi, but it had been buried under all the resentment. Now, I made every effort for it to come through. It's said that when we want to change our behavior, we should act "as if." In other words, if you lack confidence, you begin to act in a confident manner, and eventually your emotions conform to your behavior. I figured the Cuddle Offensive could only help my own emotional state. Because I still wanted Bodhi to lie down to be petted, as opposed to inserting himself between Sierra and me or just pushing himself into my space, he received no attention when he forgot himself and became pushy. But there were plenty of other opportunities to reward him, and I took full advantage.

When the Cuddle Offensive had been in full swing for a week, I began to notice a difference. Bodhi didn't seem quite as frantic about pushing himself into our faces for affection, and whenever I was petting Sierra, he seemed more willing to lie nearby and wait for me to notice and respond. Sierra was even able to enjoy the sole attention that came with being brushed while Bodhi relaxed next to me. Certainly some of this success was attributable to the fact that Bodhi was getting rewarded more often and intensely for calm behavior, but I believe it was also largely due to his finally feeling true acceptance and affection. Isn't that what we all want? Whatever the reason, something was working. The handling exercises had paid off as well, and I was eventually able to brush Bodhi without his jaws closing around my hand or the brush. I could hold his paw and inspect between his paw pads, detangle his coat, look in his ears, and check his gums. And we continued to practice restraint holds so his veterinary visits could be more pleasant for everyone.

Training was going well, too. Bodhi would now lie down from a standing or sitting position on a verbal cue alone. He was learning Go to Your Bed, and I'd started to teach him tricks. He had just started to learn Take a Bow, and had a pretty decent Spin…well, he did seem to think his feet all had to leave the ground at the same time partway through it, making it more of a spin-leap-spin, but it was cute and it became part of the trick. I had visions of him and Sierra, who already knew a few tricks, bowing and doing other tricks in tandem. But the best thing about training was that Bodhi seemed to enjoy it, and was able to maintain focus long enough to learn. It was something we could do together that was fun and productive.

As Bodhi gradually began to relax, the destruction around the house slowed. Miracle of miracles, we finally had an entire week where Bodhi hadn't destroyed anything. It was cause for celebration.

# Mush!

In addition to training the dogs and working on improving their behavior, I also wanted to find ways to keep them stimulated mentally and physically. Since Bodhi and Sierra are northern breed mixes, I pondered ways we could tap into their heritage. Siberian Huskies were used for centuries by the Chukchi tribe off the Siberian peninsula for pulling sleds, herding reindeer, and serving as watchdogs. Okay, so I've never seen reindeer around here; perhaps Santa and his sled team have avoided our home, having determined that my behavior doesn't deserve positive reinforcement. As for Sierra or Bodhi being watchdogs? Well, they're very accomplished at watching me stuff Kongs, but somehow I'm guessing that's not what the Chukchi meant. Pulling, however, is an area where I felt I could help them to engage their natural abilities. And a friend introduced me to a way to do just that.

Early one morning, as Kathy and Niko accompanied me and Sierra around the park trails, Kathy mentioned that she and her husband practiced urban mushing with Niko on the weekends. Rather than pulling a sled (we're not likely to get snow in these parts), the sport allows dogs to pull a rider on a scooter that resembles a long skateboard with a vertical pole at the front topped by handlebars. The dogs wear special body harnesses designed for the sport, and there are plenty of safety rules, including a proper dog to rider weight ratio and the need for the two-legged contingent to wear a helmet. As we walked along, I excitedly peppered Kathy with questions. She and Gary would be running Niko that weekend, she said. Why didn't I come along and bring Sierra so we could try her and Niko as a team? I agreed. We could always add Bodhi to the mix once Sierra and I got the hang of it. Since it was already Friday, I had only one day to wait.

The next morning, we met in the parking lot at 6:30 so we could get a few runs in before the weather got too warm. Kathy and Gary had brought along all of the necessary equipment, including a bicycle that Gary would be riding ahead of the dogs to encourage them to run. They took the scooter off the tow rack and showed me how to squeeze the brakes gently so I wouldn't go flying over the handlebars when I stopped. *Just like riding a bicycle*, I thought. *Gliding along good, cartwheeling bad. Check.* Gary encouraged me to take a practice run with the scooter alone first, to get a feel for it. He held it upright as I mounted it. I pushed off with one foot against the asphalt and took off across the empty parking lot, getting the feel for turning and braking. It was fun, even if I was a bit wobbly. With a smile on my face, I looped back around to where they were parked.

Next, Sierra and I stood by as the couple got Niko harnessed. They did a short loop around the dirt track with Gary riding the bike out ahead, and Niko pulling Kathy. Then it was my turn. Niko and Sierra would be pulling me. As Kathy got Sierra into her harness, Gary handed me the helmet and gloves. I had a moment to reflect on just how long it had been since I'd done anything this athletic. But the couple was encouraging and offered excellent tips, including to keep the scooter a bit to the side of the dogs as I followed so that if they slowed or stopped I wouldn't run into them. They mentioned that the dogs would likely begin to run much faster when the dirt path began to slope downward. With a combination of excitement and trepidation, I set off.

I wasn't the only one who hadn't mushed before. I was pretty certain that in her pre-adoption life Sierra hadn't done any urban mushing, so I wasn't sure what to expect. She was tethered to Niko by a short nylon rope that ran between their mushing collars. Would the two become overly aroused and get snarky with each other? They'd played before in Niko's back yard and seemed to get along just fine. Hopefully that would help. But would Sierra actually *want* to run, or would she just stand there wondering when she could go chase squirrels? And, speaking of squirrels, what if one crossed our path while the dogs were running at full speed? Would I discover what dirt tasted like?

Gary pedaled away on the bike, encouraging the dogs to chase him. Niko—he of the mucho mushing experience—began to run after the bicycle. Sierra immediately fell in alongside him. We were off! Sierra looked as though she'd been born for mushing, and I suppose that in a way she had. The dogs settled into an easy rhythm, running shoulder to shoulder as though the scooter and I were weightless. Soon we approached the downhill portion of the track. As promised, the dogs broke into a full-out dash. I gripped the handlebars and held on tight. It was scary and exhilarating all at the same time. I tried to focus on holding on, not hitting any rocks, keeping to the side of the dogs, not wiping out…Gary, still on the bike that was now barely ahead, glanced back and called out, "Relax your body!" I hadn't realized I was in a semi-crouch with every muscle clenched. Once I took a deep breath and released some of the physical tension, it became easier and a lot more fun. The speed, the wind in my hair—okay, not my hair, thanks to the helmet, but my face—felt wonderful. It looked as though the dogs were feeling pretty joyous themselves as they ran along with ears back, eyes bright, and mouths open in panting excitement. We finished the run and came to a stop near the dog park.

I dismounted. We untethered the dogs and gave them a little water and a few small pieces of cooked chicken that Kathy had brought along. Kathy wasn't a trainer, but she had great natural instincts when it came to dog behavior and training. She'd wanted to make sure Sierra had good associations with the experience. I suspected that wouldn't be a problem. We stood there chatting for a few minutes about the finer points of the run, and then let the dogs play in the park. After the short break we set out for the final run, with me on the scooter and both dogs pulling. This time we'd be taking the dirt path that eventually turned to asphalt as it led back to the parking lot.

Niko and Sierra ran a bit slower than before but maintained a nice, even pace. Dirt soon turned to pavement, and as we approached the parking area, we navigated around the parked cars of joggers and other early risers. Suddenly, the dogs darted sharply to the left and jumped up onto a grassy island. Somehow they had neglected to brief me about a sniffing detour. I turned the handlebars sharply and squeezed the brakes gently. Thankfully, I was able to maneuver the scooter around the concrete border, hence avoiding ending the day with an up-close examination of the local plant life.

All in all, it had been a great, fun adventure. Sierra had loved mushing and I had, too. I wanted to do it again. Over the next few months, C.C. and I got more and more involved in the sport. I joked to Kathy that she was my pusher, drawing me in deeper as she guided me to websites for purchasing all the necessary equipment, including a scooter of our own. Fortunately, Bodhi seemed to enjoy the activity as much as Sierra, and he too was a natural. The dogs ran well together, and soon we were regular weekend mushers. I still worry about critters running across our path, thereby short-circuiting Sierra's brain, but so far so good.

There's a lot more to the sport, of course, including teaching cues for turning left or right, and dealing with distractions. By the way, dogs don't have to be northern breeds to participate. So long as a dog is physically able and the dog-to-rider weight ratio is acceptable, any dog can mush. Check it out (www.urbanmushing.com)!

# 17

# The Queen and the Cover Boy

It's strange how the older you get, the faster time seems to fly. It's now been a little over three years since we adopted "Bazooka." Going by the vet's original estimate, he's now at least four years old! And Sierra, who was roughly a year-and-a-half to two years when we adopted her, is now five-and-a-half or even six. Not having human kids, I don't know that it's exactly the same feeling of *Where did the time go? They grow up so fast!* But I'm guessing it's very similar.

Things have improved immensely. I can now walk Bodhi past other dogs without worrying that he's going to lunge at them—and that includes dogs who are bigger than him. Upon spotting a dog who makes him nervous, he'll automatically place himself by my left side and look up at me with an expression that says he's quite pleased with himself. *I'm* certainly pleased, and will still sometimes reward him with a treat to remind him of what a great job he's doing. We've even walked past his nemesis, the Big Black Lab Formerly Known as Darth Vader, and Bodhi's behaved perfectly. Sometimes when keeping it together is especially difficult for him, he'll walk by my side while making a whining-squeaking sound. The other day as we passed Darth, Bodhi was squeaking so loudly that the owner chuckled and commented, "You really ought to oil that dog!"

Sierra never had Bodhi's reactivity issues around other dogs, but her stalking approach was a problem. I have to admit that at first I found it fascinating to watch, to the point that I didn't do anything to stop it. It was like getting a glimpse at the predator beneath the façade of a domesticated dog. But the behavior sometimes frightened other dogs and owners. It was also troublesome that once Sierra was in that hyper-focused mode, there was no getting her attention. We've put in lots of practice time at the park and now, regardless of which dog is approaching, I can call, "Sierra!" and she'll instantly turn, give me eye contact and, more often than not, come and sit right in front of me. She always was a little over-achiever.

Believe it or not, Bodhi has become a star obedience pupil! He's gotten so good, in fact, that I've taken to letting him off leash in the remote canyons of our local park. Eyes sparkling, tongue hanging out in a goofy, happy pant, he'll gallop a short distance ahead, sniff out critters, and leave pee-mail on poor, unsuspecting bushes. Then he'll dash back to my side, all but grinning, accept a treat for checking in, and, upon my release cue, take off again. Of course, that pattern was instilled with plenty of practice, first with a long line to ensure he'd keep checking in and would come immediately when called. Our hard work has paid off. Bodhi is doing *so* well that last week I was able to call him back as he was in mid-charge after a bunny! Others are giving good reports on his behavior, too. Our vet has taken to saying, "I can't believe that's the same dog!" and the groomers say his behavior is "like night and day." I love hearing it. I'm proud of my boy. Oh, and speaking of the veterinarian, once we switched both dogs to a raw food diet, Bodhi's urinary problems disappeared.

As for the destruction, I'm cautiously optimistic. Things are way better than they were, as evidenced by the fact that a few times, television remotes and even DVDs have been left on the coffee table overnight by accident, and they were still intact in the morning. Years ago, I would have been kicking myself and cursing Bodhi for destroying them. And I can now leave both dogs with indoor-outdoor access without worrying when I'm out doing daytime errands. I might be gone anywhere from 30 minutes to four hours, and nothing gets destroyed.

The lessening of destruction might seem like a natural by-product of the dogs maturing, but I don't know if that's the entire explanation, at least with regard to Bodhi. I think it has more to do with his finally—*finally!*—feeling comfortable, safe, and part of a permanent family. I believe that the structure of his life here, knowing for the most part what to expect, and the fact that *our* behavior is consistent, kind, and loving has everything to do with his becoming calmer. He's not only bonded with me, and vice-versa, but he absolutely adores C.C. I love watching both dogs become blissed out from the rubs and pets they receive from C.C. when he gets home from work. As for me, when I watch Bodhi running happily back to me across the hills at the park, I know we're connected by the best kind of leash—the invisible kind that's made of heartstrings.

Sierra is still the loving, wonderful dog she always was, but she has definitely become a bit more—well, *bitchy* toward Bodhi. I've noticed over the years having both male and female dogs, and having observed dogs belonging to friends and clients, that many females seem more manipulative, while a lot of males seem sweet, but perhaps a bit less calculating. I suppose it makes sense. Just as there is more and more research showing that human males and females actually are wired differently, male and female dogs might be as well, and each sex might have some personality traits show up more dominantly than others. Or maybe it's just my dogs. In Sierra's case, she'll do things like chew a bully stick for just a bit, wait for Bodhi to finish his, and then lie down right in front of him to finish hers. *Hah! I've still got one and you don't! Just go ahead and try to take it!* When I'm making my morning green smoothie, she'll place herself right next to me so that when I get to the Magical Banana-Cutting Moment, she'll be first in line. Of course, this never *really* puts her first in line, as I make both dogs sit and wait and they get the banana slices at the same time. But I have no doubt that in her mind, Sierra is the Queen.

We haven't been doing as much urban mushing as we'd like, due to C.C.'s work schedule and the warm weather, but we plan to pick it up again this winter. There is a new activity I've got both dogs involved in, though. A year ago, I became involved in photography. I'd always enjoyed taking photos of people, places, and, of course, animals. I had good timing and an eye for composition, but absolutely no experience with a "real" SLR camera, even back in the days of film. So when I bought a DSLR—a digital camera with interchangeable lenses—I had no clue. I didn't know an F stop from a bus stop. I had no idea about shutter speed, ISO, or any of the other technical aspects of photography. Determined to learn, I spent months immersed in online videos and books. And, of course, I put in plenty of practice. I photographed the cactus, the hillsides, our local lizards and bunnies, zoo animals, friends' dogs, rescue dogs (appealing photos helped them to get adopted faster), anything that would sit still long enough, and some that wouldn't.

My favorite subjects were, of course, Sierra and Bodhi. Say what you will about their behavior, but they're both beautiful. Sierra, like so many dogs, wasn't too sure about the camera at first. She just didn't like that giant eye pointed her way. It took some classical conditioning—pairing pointing the camera at her with a treat, then point, click, treat—to get her comfortable with it. Bodhi, on the other hand, surprised me by being a natural. The camera didn't seem to bother him at all. Over the next six months he morphed into Bodhi, Dog Model.

On our morning walks in the park, I'd let Bodhi off leash and then point to a spot on the hillside, or to a bench. He'd scramble up and stand there, or sit if I told him to, with his head raised proudly. More often than not his mouth would be open and sometimes, especially if he was tired, his long tongue would hang out. It might not have been a typical modeling pose, but it was awfully cute. I began posting photos of both dogs on Facebook, and the feedback was encouraging. I used photos of my furry models in my work, too. I wrote an article for the *Whole Dog Journal* about separation anxiety and included photos of Sierra. Appropriately enough, Sierra also ended up as the cover girl for my book, *Don't Leave Me! Step-by-Step Help for Your Dog's Separation Anxiety.* Speaking of covers, Bodhi ended up on the cover of *The Chronicle of the Dog*, the magazine of the Association of Professional Dog Trainers. How ironic is that? From Bad Boy to Cover Boy. Go, Bodhi!

When the dogs aren't working, playing, exercising, or training, their favorite thing is to get rubs and affection. Sierra still glories in her Double Crazy Legs tummy rubs, and bows to solicit attention. She'll do a deep bow and stay in that lowered stretch position as I give scratches that start at her ears and head and then move down her body. Bodhi loves his scratches and tummy rubs, too. When I rub the sides of his face with my palms as I put my head down to touch the top of his, he often lets out a deep sigh. It moves me every time, as it affirms that he's finally relaxing and feeling loved and accepted.

~ * ~ * ~ * ~ * ~ * ~ * ~ * ~ * ~ * ~ * ~ * ~ *

Yesterday was Thanksgiving, and I am reflecting on just how thankful I am for these dogs. Sierra really did pull me out of a pit of grief and turn the light back on in my heart. As for Bodhi, he certainly taught me a major lesson in patience. And—who'd have believed it—I am truly crazy about the boy. Maybe finding him on my birthday was a gift after all.

Like other Thanksgivings, C.C. and I were invited to our friends' home for dinner. There was a storm brewing, and we knew we'd be gone from mid-afternoon until mid-evening. We didn't want to lock the dogs outside in the rain, and so, after a brief discussion, we decided to leave them with indoor-outdoor access. I hoped the only stuffing we would see this year would be on our plates. I felt Bodhi had overcome his anxiety to the point that he would be able to relax and not feel the need to destroy anything. Happily, that's exactly what happened. We left at 2:30 in the afternoon and returned at 8:30 that night to find two yawning dogs and all the furniture intact.

I can't claim to have changed Bodhi into a whole other dog. He still has some issues with anxiety and insecurity that I believe are genetic. But he's come such a long way. As for Sierra, although she has her moments, she too has made amazing progress. At the beginning of this journey with Sierra and Bodhi and their myriad of behavior issues, the road ahead looked endless and, at times, very bleak. But looking back, I can see how far we all have come. And the adventure continues.

# PART II

## The Wolves

*18*

# Two Little Reds and the Big, Mostly Good Wolves

It all started with an ad in the local newspaper. C.C. and I had been looking through the classifieds for a companion for our German Shepherd Soko when the headline "Wolf Hybrid Pups" leaped out at me. My previous lupine experience had been limited to hanging out with Tubby, an alleged wolfdog who had belonged to a childhood friend. Tubby was a German Shepherd mix who spent most of his days lying beneath the kitchen table living up to his name. Sure, he was half wolf as my friend claimed—and I'm half Amazonian princess. But here I was, years later, excitedly circling an ad that filled my head with visions of adorable, wolfy-looking puppies. We made an appointment to visit the sanctuary.

Driving up the long, winding dirt road, we wondered what part-wolf, part-dog pups would act like. Would they howl? Would they be difficult to housetrain? Would we bring one home? As we parked next to a worn split-rail fence, a tall red-haired woman strode out to meet us. Tia was friendly, but had a no-nonsense manner that said she would gladly show us the pups, but she had plenty of other things to do too, so don't be wasting her time. We didn't; as it turned out, the five Husky-wolf mix pups, who were indeed adorable, were just not a good match for us. Their over-the-top, almost frantic energy would have been too much for Soko who, although friendly with other dogs, could become easily overwhelmed. Still, we spent some time interacting with the puppies, and also got to see a few adult wolfdogs. Tia explained that she didn't breed, and that in fact she spayed or neutered every animal who came into the facility. She didn't normally have puppies. She had taken the litter in because they had nowhere to go, and would place them only into qualified homes.

Tia and I were both redheads with a love of wolves, dogs, and helping animals in need. She told me about how she'd taken in the first wolfdog from her brother, and how word had quickly spread that hers was the place to bring a wolfdog if you couldn't keep it. She had ten in residence at the time. By the end of our visit, I had volunteered to come up and help her with whatever needed doing around the ten acres that made up Villalobos Rescue Center.

~ * ~ * ~ * ~ * ~ * ~ * ~ * ~ * ~ * ~ * ~ * ~ * ~ * ~ * ~ *

Over the next ten years, I made hundreds of ninety-minute drives from our San Fernando Valley home to the rural desert town of Agua Dulce. I'd quickly gone from "volunteer" to "rescue partner" to "Executive Director." The fancy title really just meant that I scooped poop, encouraged the shy wolves to be more comfortable, did some training, went out on rescue calls, assisted distraught wolfdog owners on the phone and in person, and did whatever else I could to help.

There were no volunteers in those early years. It was just Tia and me, forty or so wolves, and mountains of pea gravel and chain link. Since we were the only ones around, we did almost everything ourselves, including most of the hard physical labor. All the pens had dirt floors covered by pea gravel so the wolves could have dry, clean flooring. Since the pea gravel would get scooped up along with the poop, it had to be replenished periodically. With forty-something wolves, that meant we were constantly pea graveling. Can I just say how much I *hate* shoveling pea gravel? It's backbreaking work. We used huge, heavy shovels to scoop and dump it into a wheelbarrow. We then maneuvered the wheelbarrow into a pen, trying not to tip it along the way. Finally, we dumped it out and spread the pea gravel with a metal rake.

We had to use 9-gauge chain link panels to build the enclosures, since they're much heavier than the standard 11-gauge type. Wolves can chew through 11-gauge the way I chew through a slice of pizza. Heavier and stronger might have been better, but it wasn't much fun to carry. The enclosures sat at the top of a long, steep hill, and in those days we didn't have a vehicle that could navigate the terrain. And so, we carried the panels up ourselves. I even remember us rolling huge boulders up that sharp incline to put in one of the larger enclosures. I would later pay for those activities by requiring surgery for two double-inguinal hernias. But, at the time, it was gratifying to see the results of our labors.

In the winters, things got really tough. The hurricane force winds would blow the roofs off some of the pens, and they'd have to be rewired into place. When it stormed, flooding was a problem. One year it got so bad that Tia and I spent a full eight-hour day digging a long, wide trench through the mud in back of the enclosures so the rain would be diverted and not flood the wolves' living space. Afterward, covered in mud and poop, ready to collapse, I headed home to shower and fall into bed. But on the way, a police officer pulled me over. I'd been driving 80 mph and hadn't even noticed him behind me. Granted, he hadn't had his lights flashing, but still, it speaks to how utterly exhausted I was at the time. He took one look at me and asked what had happened. I was close to sobbing as I babbled on about wolves, rain, and flooding. The officer must have either felt sorry for me, thought I was nuts, or both. He let me off with a warning.

There were roughly forty to fifty animals at the rescue at any given time. They ranged from low content wolfdogs—mostly dog, with a bit of wolf mixed in—to pure wolves, with just about every level of wolf content in between. One resident, Max, was the only dog who had little to no wolf content. Although he was more of a Shepherd mix, Tia had taken him in out of the goodness of her heart, since he had nowhere else to go.

Due to a biological phenomenon called hybrid vigor, wolfdogs are often bigger than either wolves or dogs. One of the residents, Tiny, was certainly a shining example. Although we never weighed him, he would have easily tipped the scale at over 130 pounds. He looked like a white German Shepherd-Pyrenees-wolf cross, and had ended up at the rescue wearing the label of Chicken Killer. There were two actual wolf-Great Pyrenees crosses as well, Cujo and Renata, who had been the sanctuary's first residents. They were extremely sweet and loved attention and affection.

You might be wondering where all of these animals came from. After all, wolves aren't roaming the Hollywood hills or catching waves down at Venice Beach. Each resident had, at some point, been someone's pet. In most cases the owners had purchased a pup from a breeder, many of whom would sell to anyone with enough money regardless of whether the buyers had proper containment or any idea of what they were getting into. Although wolves and wolfdogs make for beautiful, if extremely nippy puppies, as they come into adolescence and adulthood they are often given up for acting like...well, wolves! Unlike a naughty dog who chews your bedroom slippers, high content wolfdogs and wolves have been known to eat through drywall and tear up linoleum. For this reason, many end up living in outdoor enclosures or being given up to rescue centers—that is, if the owners are lucky enough to find one that will take them. Many who are not so lucky end up euthanized. While some, like Tiny, were given up due to being a danger to small animals, for others, their only crime was that their owner no longer had the time or interest to care for them. And then there were the odd cases, like the beautiful black wolf Cochise, a favorite of mine. He had come from a woman in Las Vegas who fancied herself a witch and had wanted to somehow include Cochise in her rituals.

Tia and I both cared for the residents and did whatever else needed doing around the property. Many times while she was doing a task that required physical labor, I would spend time in the enclosures, giving each pair of wolves attention and socialization. We were well aware of how vital it was to keep the animals healthy not only physically, but emotionally. Many of the higher content wolfdogs and pure wolves were skittish of people when they first arrived. Although they had been someone's pet, some had been relegated to an outdoor pen with no attention, and some had simply never been socialized around anyone but the owners. My specialty became working with the fearful ones. I would sit in the dirt and use non-threatening body language to let them know my intentions were peaceful. Sometimes I was silent, sometimes I'd speak very quietly, and sometimes I'd sing softly, which helped to calm them. Since I knew the main sense with which canines explore the world is smell, I devised a technique to help the wolves get more comfortable with me. I would sit at one corner of the enclosure, with the wolves at the far end. Then, after a time, I'd get up and walk very slowly, giving them a wide berth to get past me to the opposite corner. They would inevitably dart past and go directly to where I'd been sitting, and sniff the ground. This allowed them to check me out without actually having to be near me. I later applied the same technique to working with dog training clients' fearful dogs in their homes. I would move from living room couch to chair, allowing the dogs to sniff where I'd sat. It helped the fearful dogs just as it did the wolves.

Because I approached the wolves with respect, rather than trying to "dominate" them or use outdated, force-based techniques, I was able to gain their trust. It was a good thing, too, since pretty much every one of them outweighed me, and all were at least twice as strong. But not a single one ever threatened me, and certainly none bit me—that is, except for Cherokee. And it was my own fault. Cherokee shared a pen with a shy female wolfdog who I absolutely adored. One freezing cold winter day, I passed by the pen and saw my girl at the back. Cherokee was standing somewhere in the middle, glaring at me as usual. (Tia and her daughter Tania seemed to be the only humans he would tolerate.) I placed my knuckle through the chain link and called her name softly, trying to coax her over to lick my hand as she sometimes did. In a flash, Cherokee was at the fence. He sank his teeth into the joint of my knuckle and pulled. He was at the back of the pen before I could register the damage. It had all happened in a matter of seconds. Although the cold stopped me from feeling much pain at the time, blood was dripping from my hand. I started down the hill back to the house. Tia's husband at the time was always concerned about someone suing them over being injured on the property, especially with the wolves there. I knew he was at home, so I draped my sweatshirt over my bloody hand, passed him in the hallway, did my best to call out a cheery greeting, and headed for the bathroom. I cleaned the wound, told Tia what had happened, and went home. Later that night, she told me on the phone that her husband had walked into the bathroom afterwards and exclaimed, "Where did all this blood come from?" I hadn't realized I'd left such a mess. I can't remember what excuse she gave him, but I'm sure it was a creative one.

I thought I had disinfected the wound, but apparently, I hadn't done the best job. There was some swelling at the site, but I assumed that was normal. I was working in an office at the time and, a few days later, one of my co-workers commented that my hand looked awfully swollen. The swelling had crept from my knuckle up my hand, and now even my wrist was swollen. "You really need to get to a doctor," she said. She was right. I visited the urgent care center at the hospital. The doctor on duty examined my hand and asked what had happened. I knew I couldn't tell her. Any time a bite from an unfamiliar animal is reported, the hospital must report it to the police, and animal control is also informed. That was the last thing I wanted. And so, I told her I'd been bitten by a dog. She looked at me dubiously. "A dog?" she asked. "What kind?" "A big one," I responded. Fortunately, she let it go at that, and prescribed a round of antibiotics. From that time on that, I admired Cherokee's pen mate from a distance while she was with him.

# 19

# Wolf Sitting, Pit Bulls
# and Unusual Humans

Tia always had great instincts when it came to the wolves. She had an intuitive sense of which ones would get along, which made pairing them up much easier. And although she didn't have formal training, she was an excellent trainer as well. She was so good, in fact, that she began doing film work. Wolves are not the easiest animals to train. They don't do things just because you want them to, or, sometimes, even because you have food. But Tia could get them to do "pack runs" from point A to point B, which came in handy for films, television, and commercials. I remember a music video she did for a beautiful singer where a wolf had to walk slowly past a bonfire as the woman sat there singing and strumming a guitar. Getting a wolf to walk slowly past fire—a natural fear trigger—is no easy feat. She could also get two or three of the wolves to jump on people, to make it look as though they were taking someone down; for everyone's safety, she'd often double for the star. One summer, she was off in Costa Rica filming one of the Jungle Book movies. I was thrilled that Spirit, one of the wolfdogs I was closest with, would be going. Poor Spirit had come into the rescue as a senior with a collar embedded in her neck because the owner couldn't get near her to adjust it as she grew up. It had to be surgically removed. Now, here she was, a movie star! Her job was to grab a main character's hat off his head. It was a cute trick, and it looked great on film.

While Tia was off filming, since I still lived over an hour away, she asked another friend to come and do the basic daily maintenance of feeding and watering. I would, of course, come up as well. The only problem was Roxy. Roxy was a pure wolf, and there was no middle ground with her: she either loved you or detested you. If you fell into the latter category, watch out! Fortunately, she adored Tia and me. But the woman who came to do the feeding couldn't even get in the pen with her. I asked C.C. whether he would mind if we babysat Roxy at our house for the summer. He was used to unusual requests by that time, and not only agreed but, with my assistance, built the enclosure in our back yard that would be Roxy's summer home. We used chain link panels, of course, and then paver stones for the flooring. A wooden dog house completed *Chez Roxy*. I rotated things she could chew on and explore and, of course, I spent lots of time each day in the pen with her. That she wanted my company at 4:00 a.m., as evidenced by her howling outside our bedroom window, was not a good thing. Other than that, it worked out fine. The only problem came when it was time to drive her back up to the rescue. I had a crate waiting by the car. I attached a leash and started to walk her out through the side yard to the front of the house. Just then a car went past, blaring its horn. Roxy panicked and began jerking to and fro on the leash like a kite in a high wind. I had been carrying hot dogs, and tried to wave one under her nose to get her attention. She looked at me as if to say, *Aren't you the one who's been telling people a fearful animal over threshold isn't interested in food?* Oh, yeah. Right. Fortunately, I managed to get her crated and into the car without further incident.

Both Tia and I felt strongly about doing educational programs. We would bring a few of the wolfdogs and visit various animal control agencies, where we'd teach the officers about wolf behavior and give suggestions on how to deal with wolfdogs so no one would get hurt. We visited school classrooms with a wolfdog and taught the children about wolves, and how they belong in the wild, not in people's homes. And every year for twelve years, we had a booth at America's Family Pet Expo, where thousands of people would attend over the weekend. We'd hang posters, distribute educational materials, and sell everything from T-shirts to wolf head erasers to raise funds. Making sure the animals we brought along were safe and comfortable was our first priority, of course. While it could be challenging at times, it was never as exhausting as talking with people from sunup to sundown. Many stopped by to tell us about their own wolfdogs. Others, apparently missing the point, asked when we were going to breed a litter so they could buy a puppy. The pet fair was hard work, but hopefully some education reached receptive ears.

Over time Tia began to get more and more involved with Pit Bulls. She'd always had her own, but now increasing numbers were coming in as rescues. Although all the animals were still on her property, we divided the responsibilities: she would handle the Pit Bull side of things, and I would deal with the wolves. Part of that entailed all the wolf-related phone calls coming to my house. You might not think there would be that many, but during the summers, when people tend to dump dogs, there could be as many as ten calls a day. Almost all of the callers wanted to give their animals up. If we had room at the rescue, which could happen due to a resident passing of old age or a very low content wolfdog being adopted out, I would speak with the person for a long time and get as much information as I could. I quickly learned the importance of asking for photos. I still have the first photo anyone ever sent me of a wolf who needed rescuing: it turned out to be a Golden Retriever.

When the rescue center was full, which was most of the time, placement assistance became challenging. I would have been happy to refer people to other sanctuaries in the area if there had been any, but there weren't. As a result, I spent a lot of time traveling to people's homes and, free of charge, helping them with training, showing them how to raise their fencing or to build proper enclosures, and generally doing everything possible to help them keep their pet. As every rescuer knows, although it is immensely satisfying to be able to help, there is a lot of heartache that goes with the territory.

Then there were the people who got nasty when I couldn't help them. I distinctly remember the woman who called at 4:30 in the morning. She wanted me to drive three hours away, right then and there, to get a wolf she couldn't keep any more. When I explained nicely that it was the middle of the night and I would call her back in the morning, she spat a string of curses at me and hung up.

Emails came in daily from folks who wanted a place for their wolfdog to go, or had behavioral questions or requests. Some of the requests were a bit odd. There was the woman who wanted to adopt a wolf to pull her wheelchair. Another wanted to do sheep herding with a pure wolf. A man wrote that he enjoyed my wolfdog book, and that his wolfdog did too, so much so that he had eaten it. But other emails were stranger, and sometimes humorous in an unintentional way. There was one that started, "Hi, our family dog is a mix of pure bred Alaskan Malamute and Blonde Bobtail Timber Wolf." Yes, you read that right, and no, there is no such thing as a Blonde Bobtail Timber Wolf, or, for that matter, a Black Mountain Megawolf or any of the other crazy names some breeders make up for their own lines. Another inquiry came from a woman who wanted to know whether subordinates in a pack ever sleep with the alpha members. It seems that her wolfdog slept on her side of the bed, not her husband's, and she wanted to know if that proved she was the alpha in their family.

If that's not weird enough, one woman emailed, "I am writing because my ex-husband has a wolf costume that he wears around his house. This is not a joke. I am very concerned about this because he has my kids every other weekend. Can you please help me to find more information?" Not being a psychologist, that one was out of my jurisdiction. On a similar note, a man who lived with a pack of eleven wolves asked my opinion on something he was considering. The wolves all lived together in a large fenced area in back of his house. Each morning he would step out his back door and they'd run over to greet him. He had noticed that as he put his head down, they would all rub and nuzzle against his face. But one seemed afraid, and wouldn't come quite as close. What was the best type of material, he wanted to know, for creating a wolf mask? He planned to wear the mask over his face during greetings, as he believed that would get the reticent one to see that he was one of them. I politely explained why I didn't think it was the best course of action, hung up, and shook my head.

But the prize for the strangest email ever has to go to the art student from Stockholm who said he was working on a project about the myth of the werewolf. He'd discovered through his research that one of the ways one could become a werewolf was by drinking warm wolf milk. He wanted to create an art project where people could drink wolf milk, because although you might not think it would turn you into a werewolf, if you didn't try, how would you know? He was writing to ask whether it was possible to get some wolf milk. Had I not seen that he had also addressed the email to a number of other legitimate wolf rescues and research centers, I would have thought it was a joke. I wrote back saying that we spay and neuter and certainly don't have any wolf milk. I suggested that he consider, however, in case his project was a success, having silver bullets on hand.

*Me, Lurch, and Tia teaching a class for Animal Control officers.*
*Lurch was low on wolf content but high on personality!*

*Me with Cochise, one of my favorite males at Villalobos.*

*Me and my special girl Spirit. She came into the rescue at age ten with a collar embedded in her neck that had to be surgically removed.*

*Behind our annual wolf/wolfdog education table at America's Family Pet Expo with stars Nashaka, Spirit and Lobo.*

*The cover of our Villalobos holiday card. L to R: Nashaka, me, Tia, Duke.*

*Roxy at our house, where C.C. and I wolf-sat her one summer.*

*The wolf (L) we chased through North Hollywood and her mate (R) in the shelter awaiting transport to another wildlife sanctuary.*

*Phantom—the reason I ended up with three wolves—and his Jolly Ball with holes drilled so treats could fall out.*

*My girl Sequoia and her bone. That's HER bone to you.*

*Heyoka, me and Sequoia. Heyoka arrived with major fear issues. This much closeness was really something for him.*

*My, Phantom, what big teeth you have!*
*And my, how long it took to be able to inspect them!*

*Heyoka atop the high table in the enclosure. Such a tough life!*

Despite all of the craziness, and the hardships involved in caring for the animals on a day-to-day basis, there were fun times, too. One Christmas, Tia and I decided to send out a card from the rescue center to friends and supporters. We took Tia's favorite Pit Bull Duke, and Nashaka, one of my wolfdog buddies, and headed out to Vazquez Rocks. The majestic, reddish colored rock formations look a lot like parts of Arizona, and provided a beautiful backdrop. We weren't exactly dressed for hiking but managed, in our heels and our version of holiday clothes, to climb up to a flat rock. Tia posed with Duke by her side and Nashaka sat by me. People had always assumed Tia and I were sisters, since we were not only together so often, but we had the same long red hair and a similar facial bone structure. Even my mother had commented on the resemblance. Now, posing back to back, we did look a bit like mirror images. It was fun to see the card hanging on the walls of our local vet's office and other places around town.

As Tia got more and more involved with Pit Bulls, that part of the rescue took over. The word was out that Villalobos was an excellent Pit Bull rescue, and soon she had 150 dogs on the premises! Fortunately, they, unlike the wolves, could be adopted out. Over the years, more and more people started volunteering to work with the dogs. It seemed bizarre to me that no one ever seemed to want to work with the wolves. Of course, Tia had always been their saving grace, but other than her, she'd tell me sadly, "You're the only one who's ever cared about the wolves."

Having been a youth gang counselor earlier in life, Tia had a soft spot not only for animals who needed help, but for people who were in need of rehabilitation. She began taking on volunteers who had served time in prison, giving them a second chance just as she'd given to the dogs. Eventually, Hollywood came calling, and the reality show *Pit Bulls & Parolees* was created. I was invited to participate in an episode early on where I taught some of the parolees how to work with the dogs on hand targeting and other things that would help the fearful ones. Unfortunately, the segment was cut for time and didn't end up airing, but it was a great experience. The show is still running on Animal Planet, and it's excellent.

Tia eventually ended up moving to New Orleans with the Pit Bulls, and a man who was starting a new wolf rescue took the wolves. But before that happened, three of those wolves came home to live with C.C. and me.

# 20

# House for Sale: Three Bedrooms, Two Baths, Three Wolves

Although I was constantly learning more about wolves and wolfdogs while co-running the rescue center, I wanted to increase my knowledge from a variety of sources. And so began my travels. I visited everywhere from official wolf education centers to wolfdog rescues that had lofty names like National Wolfdog Rescue but would have more appropriately been called So-and-So's Back Yard. Some were clean, well-run sanctuaries operated by knowledgeable people, while others had well meaning owners but horrible conditions. Poor C.C. often got dragged along on these trips. We'd be planning a vacation to Arizona, and I'd say, "Hey, look, there's a rescue center not far from where we'll be staying!" Or, "I know someone who says we can visit their place while we're in the mountains!" These side trips became so commonplace that C.C. started asking in advance where I would be dragging him on our next alleged vacation.

Knowing what I did about wolves and wolfdogs and their care, I preferred to get my "fix" by working and hanging out with them at Villalobos. I certainly wasn't planning to adopt any of the rescue's residents. Our rented house in the San Fernando Valley was a relatively quiet, peaceful sanctuary and we liked it that way. Then one day a wolf named Phantom came into my life. A young man named Dewey, who lived in a quiet, suburban neighborhood, had been brokering pure wolves. He would buy a wolf for $500 from a breeder in North Dakota, have it shipped to southern California, and then sell it for $1000 to anyone who could afford it—no questions asked. The wolfdog community is a small place and Tia knew Dewey. She was aware that he had sold Phantom three times already, only to have him returned each time because he was extremely fearful and would not allow anyone to touch him. His penchant for jumping six-foot fences in a single bound didn't help.

Since Tia knew that the eight wolves who were living in Dewey's back yard would likely eventually need help, she put me in touch with him so we could keep tabs. The first day I entered the makeshift chain link enclosure that ran the length of his house, I saw a variety of beautiful wolves and a few wolfdogs. A grey and white male Malamute-wolf mix stood atop a ramshackle dog house and barked. Other younger, wolfier-looking animals shied away or took refuge at the back of the enclosure. A few of the wolves who remained nearby or came up to sniff were pure black, and I wondered if they were related. One of those gorgeous black, green-eyed creatures was Phantom. He and I spied each other right away. It was that "eyes locking across a crowded room" thing, only with less staring, as that would have made Phantom nervous. He was a large adolescent wolf, tall and a bit gawky, with long black fur and glowing green eyes. It was love at first sight, and it was mutual. I was soon sitting on the ground stroking his surprisingly thick, coarse fur and getting slobbery face kisses. Dewey walked over, looked from me to Phantom, and exclaimed, "Well, that's never happened before!" Just like dogs, wolves pick their people. I'll never know why Phantom picked me, but I'm forever grateful that he did.

I visited Dewey every few weeks and enjoyed spending time with him and the wolves. But a few months later, he received an order from the Department of Animal Control to get rid of the wolves. Dewey was divorced, and his ex-wife had contacted the Department of Child Services. She just didn't think wolves and small children mixed. Go figure. Unfortunately, by that time, Tia absolutely did not want to take in any more wolves. We were already at capacity, while still receiving countless phone calls daily. Still, for Phantom's sake, I begged her to take him in. She agreed, on the condition that it was only temporary, and that C.C. and I would find a way to house him as soon as possible. If not, he would have to be euthanized.

C.C. and I had been looking to buy our first home anyway, and we soon found the perfect place. The four-acre property showcased a three bedroom, ranch-style home that sat atop a hill surrounded by desert brush. A huge cactus spanned the front of the house. The location was peaceful, quiet, and, best of all, only twenty minutes from the rescue center. We bought it. One of the first things we did was to convert a few of the horse stalls that sat at the bottom of the property into a small wolf enclosure. Tia wanted Phantom to come and live with us as soon as possible. She knew how attached he had become to me, and reported that without me there, he was miserable and petrified of the world. She said it was heartbreaking to see. With that motivation, we got the construction on the enclosure done in record time, and Phantom was transported to his new home.

Wolves are social animals, and as much as Phantom and I were bonded, he needed canine companionship, too. Tia was only too happy for me to take another wolf or two home, and I chose the ones I felt were most in need of personal attention. Sequoia was a lovely, low-content, female Samoyed-wolf mix. At the rescue, whenever I would clean pens or sit with one of the other residents, she would stand on her hind legs in her pen and plaster her paws up against the front gate like a prisoner pleading, "Let me out!" or at least, "Come rub my tummy!" The sorrowful look on Sequoia's expressive face clinched the deal. The furry, attention-seeking missile was first on my list. Heyoka, her three-year-old male pen-mate, was 75% or so wolf mixed with Malamute. I wouldn't normally consider putting two unfamiliar males of the same age together because of the likelihood of aggression, but I knew the temperaments of both Heyoka and Phantom, and felt confident they would get along. Our pen at home was expanded to become a proper enclosure, and the three soon became a pack. Phantom and Heyoka got along just fine, with Heyoka in the role of wise leader and Phantom, the eternal bratty teenager who would grudgingly get in line when reprimanded. As for Sequoia, she gave new meaning to the term *alpha bitch*. She might have had less wolf content than the others, but she ruled those boys!

Phantom and Heyoka were roughly three to four years old when they came to live with us, and Sequoia, around six. With lots of time, love, and patience, the wolves and I built bonds of trust that would last for the ten years they spent here. That's not to say there weren't plenty of challenges along the way.

# 21

# Who's Afraid of the Big Black Brat?

Attempting to house wolves can best be described in two words: extremely challenging. We started out with a set of horse stalls that measured approximately 30 x 70 feet and had a corrugated metal roof. At our request, a handyman sawed away most of the metal stall dividers. To make the enclosure dig-proof, we first tried using a three-foot-wide skirting around the inside perimeter. But the wolves quickly began tunneling themselves a condo beneath it. So we switched to the wall-to-wall version, covering every square inch of the ground with chain link. A layer of dirt went over the chain link, and the final layer was pea gravel. The spaces between the edges of the metal roof and the sides of the pen were sealed with more chain link and, for good measure, a hot wire was set up around the top inner perimeter. Finally, a perimeter fence, complete with chains and padlocks, was erected a few feet out surrounding the entire enclosure.

You might wonder why we went to all of that trouble. Another two words: escape artists! People are often surprised at how easily wolves can dig their way under, jump over, or eat their way through pretty much anything in their path. Again, most wolves I've seen can chew through 11-gauge chain link like a knife going through butter. We might have gone above and beyond with the intensity of our preparations, but we were definitely ready. It was the Fort Knox of wolfdom.

Feeding wasn't exactly easy, either. Oh, sure, we could have just given them some dog kibble and been done with it, but the wolves' nutrition was very important to me. I wanted to do it right. We put them on what is referred to as a BARF diet...an appetizing acronym, I know. It stands for Bones and Raw Food and, for our wolves, the main staple was raw chicken backs. I would visit the butcher every two weeks and bring home two forty-pound boxes of frozen chicken backs. Each time I entered the store it felt like the start of a joke: A vegetarian walks into a butcher shop…Oh, and did I mention *frozen*? During the winters, C.C. and I would stand out in the freezing cold, breaking up solid blocks of chicken and then placing the pieces into freezer bags, which would then go into the meat freezer. I'd have plastic bags at the ready as C.C., with a crowbar, tried to pry the chicken pieces apart. I would pull some of the meat apart with my glove-covered hands as well. Imagine how much fun it was to do this every two weeks! At some point we finally realized that if we let the meat thaw overnight, the process would be at least a little bit easier.

Then there was the maintenance. Pea gravel, as previously mentioned, serves as an excellent ground cover. It keeps dirt and dust to a minimum, and can be easily hosed down. Unfortunately, thousands of those little pea-sized rocks had to be trucked in, dumped outside the enclosure, and then shoveled into a wheelbarrow. The wheelbarrow would then be rolled through the narrow enclosure gate, where the gravel would be poured out and evenly spread with a metal rake, just as Tia and I did at the rescue center. This required some serious elbow grease. C.C. and I did most of the work and, on occasion, my friend Leslie came by to lend a hand. Because bits of pea gravel would be scooped away daily along with the poop, it had to be replenished regularly.

I've described all the trouble we went to in order to care for the wolves so you'll have an inkling of how I felt after a troubling incident occurred. But first, you should know that although I'd always been able to pet Phantom, that didn't mean I could handle him like a dog. Possessing a temperament that could best be described as that of a sweet yet bratty teenager, Phantom had begun to exhibit testing behavior upon arrival. He would walk up behind me as stealthily as his large, gangly body would allow, and grab at the ponytail holder in my hair. He'd shove me gently with his shoulder as he walked by. He'd nip at my clothing. It was natural; wolves test each other to see how much they'll put up with, and they do it to people, too. I knew something had to be done before it escalated. And so, any time Phantom started the behavior, I'd give a sigh and a look of disgust and leave the pen. The idea was to teach him that doing those things resulted in the loss of a valued resource—namely, me. It was like giving him a time out, with me leaving instead of trying to get him to sit in the corner and repeat, *I am not a big bad wolf, I am not a big, bad wolf*….This non-confrontational technique was, I felt, the best way to address the situation and, given Phantom's size, strength, and potential for physical damage, it was also the safest. Unfortunately, it wasn't quite as effective as I'd hoped.

It was yet another day where the forecast called for blue skies and mountains of pea gravel. Leslie and I had been shoveling and raking for hours, and we needed a break. Leslie stood outside the enclosure drinking water while I remained inside. We chatted lazily about this and that, not at all anxious to get back to work. Suddenly, I felt a crushing pain in the back of my knee. I spun around to see Phantom, Heyoka, and Sequoia standing a few feet away. They were lined up side by side, each wearing an identical, *Who, me?* expression of innocence. But I knew the bite had come from Phantom. *Really? After all I'd done for him?* It was an irrational thought, but I couldn't help it. I was irate. Drawing myself up to my full five foot two inch height, I stormed over to him and yelled a string of words that should never, ever be used in polite company. My goal was for him to look down and away to indicate that he was deferring to me. Hah! *That* didn't happen. Now, nowhere in my two books about wolfdogs do I suggest that in a situation like this you should "Corner the offender and, while hovering over him and glaring, curse a blue streak that will have your neighbors wondering whether they need to call the police." And yet, that is exactly what I did. My usual gentle, positive training approach had taken a leave of absence, along with my sanity. I stood over Phantom with a crazy gleam in my eyes, and cursed and stared him down. Finally, he looked away. (*Note*: Do *not* try this at home with a wolf or even a dog. Really, it's just plain stupid.)

With my dignity considerably more intact than my leg, I huffed and puffed my way out of the pen and up the long staircase that led to the house. I shed my jeans and held a bag of frozen peas to the back of my knee. There were no puncture wounds, but the tissue had been crushed. I would soon be sporting a large black and blue golf ball-sized projection. I took a few deep breaths and, at Leslie's suggestion, a few drops of Rescue Remedy, a flower essence blend. Mixed in water, the solution has a calming effect. Who knew it worked so well in tequila?

Days passed, and with them came the return of my sanity and my usual calm demeanor. I knew Phantom hadn't intended to injure me; if he had, the damage would have been much, much worse. But something had to change. The next time he came up behind me and grabbed at my hair, I calmly turned and wrapped my palm over the top of his muzzle. I looked him in the eye and, in a low voice, said, "Don't." He realized that I meant it and backed off immediately. This is not something I would ever recommend that anyone do, and it's certainly not a "training method." But I was Phantom's last chance before being euthanized. I *had* to be able to interact with him, and I instinctively felt the maneuver would work. After that, our relationship gradually improved, and I began to work with him on accepting being handled. We made slow, steady progress and, within a few months, I was able to touch his paws, his teeth, and anything else that needed handling—for the most part. Phantom would always be a pure wolf, and having started this sort of desensitization before the age of three months, rather than three years, certainly would have been helpful. But over time we developed a trusting, balanced relationship that lasted for the rest of his long, sweet, bratty life.

# 22

# Heyoka Visits the Vet

Heyoka hadn't eaten for four days. Although wolves in the wild can go for a few days in a row without eating, this captive wolfdog normally went after raw chicken the way his wild cousins pursued the live variety. Something was definitely wrong.

Allowing us to check his temperature or do anything else that involved physical manipulation was out of the question. Being three quarters wolf and already three or four years old when he came to us, Heyoka had always been the most skittish of the three. Wolves are naturally afraid of people, and Heyoka's DNA ran close to his roots. He would allow gentle petting through the chain link, and sometimes even when I was inside the enclosure, so long as Phantom was positioned between us. But even then only his chest and, at times, the side of his face were fair game. The saddest part was that Heyoka really craved affection; he just wasn't comfortable with being touched. Whenever I gave Phantom scratches and tummyrubs, Heyoka would watch. Conflicted, he'd lope over to a section of chain link and rub his long, silver and white, thickly furred body against it like a cat, his eyes closed in pleasure. The cold metal substitute for human touch would have to be enough. I respected Heyoka's hands-off policy, and would never force contact on him. But when he hadn't eaten for the fourth day in a row, there was no getting around a veterinary visit.

As you might imagine, getting a rescued mostly-wolf into a crate is no simple matter. Crates are confining, and since Heyoka had never been acclimated to one, it appeared to him as a potential trap. Add to that the fact that each time he'd been crated in the past it had meant relocation, and it wasn't hard to understand his fear. The problem was that when Heyoka was truly afraid, he would fight for his life. We'd found that out the hard way early on when a vet visit had been required. My friends Michelle, Tia, and Tia's daughter Tania had come over to wrangle Heyoka into a crate. We all knew I couldn't be part of the capture. If my fur-kid lost trust in me it was all over, as I was his one safe harbor. The three women were in the enclosure's built-in catch pen for over half an hour. They used large wooden panels to create a smaller and smaller space until Heyoka would have no choice but to take refuge in the crate. At least that was the plan. Michelle told me afterwards that Heyoka had managed to jump over the barricade they'd created and had gone for her throat. This news was especially disconcerting coming from Michelle, who tended to downplay any type of drama.

After that, attempting another capture was out of the question. We decided that instead, Heyoka would be injected with a sedative so he could be placed safely into the crate and then transported to the vet's office. I was able to pick up a needle full of ketamine from the vet who normally dealt with the rescue center's wolves. The problem was, I'd never administered an injection and I wasn't about to practice on Heyoka. I racked my brain for someone who might be willing and able to help. I remembered that Michelle used to be a nurse. Unfortunately, she'd been battling cancer for years, and was currently on oxygen and living part time in a wheelchair. I called her husband Bruce to ask whether he might have any other suggestions.

During our conversation, I heard a wan voice in the background say, "I'm going over there!"

"That's not Michelle, is it?" I asked incredulously.

"Yep," sighed Bruce. "She wants to come over and give Heyoka the injection."

While I was grateful and very touched, given Michelle's health and the fact that the couple lived over an hour away, it didn't seem to be the best option. But there was no talking her out of it. A few hours later, Bruce and Michelle appeared, oxygen canister in tow.

Michelle and I stood at the top of the staircase that led down to the pen. The men, who would only scare Heyoka by virtue of their testosterone, waited on the porch.

"Are you sure you can do this?" I asked with concern.

"It's fine," Michelle replied. "I can be without the oxygen for a couple of minutes, it's no big deal."

We made our way down the stairs and into the pen. Heyoka was lying in the catch pen with his hip close to the chain link. Although weak, he could still be extremely dangerous, so delivering the injection from inside the catch pen was not possible. We entered the enclosure. Heyoka's chest rose and fell in a regular rhythm. He appeared to be lightly dozing.

Picking her way across the pea gravel as quietly as possible, Michelle approached the catch pen. As I stood watching, she rolled up her sleeve and placed her palms together in a quick, silent prayer. She then stuck her arm through a diamond in the chain link and plunged the needle gently but firmly into Heyoka's thigh. He flinched and raised his head slightly, but did not whip around to try to bite, as I'd feared he might. I released a breath I hadn't realized I'd been holding. Once Heyoka was unconscious, Bruce and C.C. lifted him into a crate and loaded him into my Jeep.

Heyoka was still knocked out when C.C. and I got to the vet's office, and the techs were able to draw blood. Because our usual vet wasn't available, we saw Dr. Renner. I don't know if it was my bringing this particular wolf in from my home rather than from the rescue center that rubbed her the wrong way, but she felt inclined to share her opinion: "I'd have put him down a long time ago," she snapped. "He'll be very difficult to handle once he's awake, you know." (My, what a charming bedside manner you have!) Once she'd gotten *that* off her chest, she conducted an examination and recommended that we leave Heyoka at the clinic overnight for observation. I reluctantly agreed. Dogs and cats are normally kept in the building's back area in metal barred cages with simple latch closures. I explained to her that the staff would need to padlock the cage or somehow make it more secure. After another glare from Doc Friendly, we left.

The next afternoon we received a call to come and pick up Heyoka. The caller sounded frazzled, but I put that down to the frantic pace of the veterinary office. Once there, we were shuttled directly into an exam room. Dr. Renner strode in.

"It was a pretty funny thing that happened here," the vet said brusquely, by way of greeting. "One of the techs opened the clinic this morning and there was your wolf, standing right in the middle of the lobby! He ate his way through four bags of our meal supplements, but worse," she chuckled, "I think the tech about shit himself!"

I was not amused. Had the tech left the front door open a fraction of a second too long, Heyoka would have been gone, and it's highly doubtful that anyone would have ever caught him. He might have starved to death slowly or been hit by a car. Hilarious, eh? After ascertaining that they had no idea what was wrong with Heyoka, and saying that they weren't too concerned since he was now clearly hungry, I asked, "Where is he?"

"Oh, they've got him downstairs in the holding area," Dr. Renner answered. "The techs just need to get him back into the crate. Why don't you go wait in the reception area."

*Oh, boy,* I thought. *The techs have no idea what they're in for.* I offered to go downstairs to help and tried to explain why, but was summarily dismissed with a wave of the vet's hand.

This particular veterinary office had seen a lot of the rescue's animals over the years. None had ever fazed the burly gang members-turned-vet-techs. These guys had wrangled huge Pit Bulls, wolves, and everything in between. But they hadn't met Heyoka. C.C. and I watched from the waiting room as a dark-haired, twenty-something tech strode confidently toward the holding area in the back. Ten minutes later, he emerged covered in a thin film of sweat, and called for another tech to assist him. The two disappeared. Fifteen minutes later they both reappeared looking sweaty, disheveled, and with a distinct deficiency in the swagger department. "We need the catch pole," one panted to a third tech, who looked at them and asked, "You wrestling alligators back there or what?" Three techs and thirty minutes later, Heyoka was safely back in the crate.

Relieved to be out of the clinic, we drove Heyoka home. On the way, we reflected on how everything is amplified with wolves and wolfdogs, especially the difficulty in handling and medical care. We never did find out what had been wrong with Heyoka, but from that day on, he began eating again as though nothing had ever happened.

# 23

# Wolves on the Loose!

It was a freezing cold winter day, and southern California was doing what a friend likes to call "storming its ass off." I was down with a case of bronchitis, watching the rain blow sideways and feeling sorry for myself. A spoonful of warm oatmeal was halfway to my mouth when the phone rang. "There's two wolves loose," Tia said breathlessly. "They got out of a woman's yard in Tarzana and they're running around in that big plant nursery. Raquel's already headed down there." So much for rest and a warm breakfast.

As I raced down to the Valley, passing drivers who didn't seem to understand it's possible to drive faster than fifteen miles an hour in the rain, I thought about the scene that might await. The nursery, popular for its huge selection of trees, plants, and gardening materials, spanned two entire city blocks and was surrounded by a six-foot chain link fence. The vast amount of square footage would make it challenging to capture a dog, never mind two wolves. Hopefully there would be a smaller enclosed area inside that they could be herded into. I knew Raquel would have her catch rope with her, and some hot dogs. A catch rope is a length of rope, like a jump rope, that's been knotted to create a loop that can easily widen or tighten. The loop gets tossed over the dog's head, similar to a cowboy roping a steer. When the end of the rope is pulled, the loop becomes smaller, tightening around the neck. I'd kept mine since my days of working at the city animal shelter. Like so many other employees, I had a "lucky" rope. When you work with animals who have the potential to cause serious injury, you become superstitious about those kinds of things. Now the rope sat next to me on the passenger seat along with a variety of wolf-enticing treats. I felt confident that between Raquel and me, we could catch the furry escapees.

The angels assigned to watch over sick, sniffly redheads were obviously on the job, because I found a parking spot close to the nursery entrance. Two Animal Control trucks were parked there as well. I spied Raquel's old red Jeep Cherokee, cousin to my hunter green one, further down the block. Raquel, a sturdy, attractive, part Native American woman in her thirties, was quite wolf-savvy. She'd lived with wolfdogs for years, and often assisted the rescue center by transporting wolves, evaluating them at shelters, and performing other helpful tasks. Like me, she often took part in emergency calls. "The police were here but they left," she told me, clearly annoyed. "They couldn't do squat. They actually scared the silver one so bad he jumped the fence. He's gone. So they called in Animal Control." At least they hadn't shot the animals. Teeth chattering, I asked what the plan was. Pulling up her parka hood, Raquel said, "We're waiting for the Animal Control vet with the dart gun. They won't let us into the nursery because we're just *citizens*." We exchanged a knowing look. We might be citizens, but we were also almost certainly the only ones with extensive experience in catching wolves.

All of us—me, Raquel, and four large, solidly built male Animal Control officers—stood huddled against the rain and wind. We waited. And waited. Finally, after a long, cold twenty minutes, the vet arrived. He knew Raquel and me, but apologetically advised us to wait outside so no legal protocol would be violated. Armed with his dart gun, he and the officers headed into the nursery. Frustrated and worried for the wolf, Raquel and I remained outside. It was impossible to see what was happening, but every now and then we'd hear a shout: "Over there! I see it!" or, "No, no, it went the other way!" After what seemed like an interminable wait, the men returned, looking a bit worse for the wear. "We cornered it," one panted, "but it jumped the fence." Raquel and I both sighed. What else would you expect a cornered wolf to do? Apparently the wolf had jumped the fence before the vet could dart her.

What happened next was straight out of an action adventure film. The vet and Animal Control officers each ran to their trucks, and Raquel and I raced to our Jeeps. The officers had an idea of the direction the wolf was headed, so we peeled out after them, tires squealing. We all zigzagged through busy Los Angeles traffic, swerving and sliding, trying to keep up. Block after block flew by. A blur of shops and warehouses quickly gave way to suburban homes. Wait! There she was, a large, black and silver wolf streaking silently down the middle of a wide, busy thoroughfare known as Victory Boulevard. Drivers stopped in their tracks, eyes a-goggle. I wondered whether they thought they were hallucinating. At least they'd have an interesting story to tell around the dinner table.

Although the wolf wasn't in a full-out run, she was still moving plenty fast. We followed the hazy silver shape as best we could through the sheets of rain, making sudden U-turns and other careening maneuvers no safety-minded driver would ever dream of making. We were all completely caught up in the chase, all thoughts of our own safety cast aside. Finally, the wolf turned up a wide residential street and slowed to a walk. We all turned the corner after her. The animal control trucks passed her and came to a stop further down the block. The officers jumped to the sidewalk, catch poles at the ready. Raquel and I hung back on opposite sides of the street, catch ropes in hand, ready to loop her if she reversed direction. The wolf looked at the officers ahead, glanced back at us, and then sprinted past the men, across the street and down the block. We all ran back to our vehicles and peeled out again in pursuit.

The rain became a torrential downpour. We could barely make out the road, much less where the wolf was headed. After what seemed like an hour of frenzied driving that should only be attempted in a video game, we spied a blurry figure turning into a narrow alleyway. By this time we were all freezing cold and exhausted, and the officers were happy to have our assistance. As they parked their trucks across the alley entrance, they instructed us to block the other end with our vehicles. That accomplished, we each stood with our wolf-catching equipment at the ready. Each officer had a snare pole as well as catch ropes, and we soggy citizens, of course, had our own catch ropes. The vet had his dart gun in hand, but at the moment, the wolf was moving too quickly to get a clean shot.

Raquel and I stood approximately twenty yards apart. The wolf ran past me, and my loop brushed the fur of her neck. Damn! I'd missed. She ran past one of the officers, with the same results. Now the wolf was beginning to get panicky. Time after time she ran past one of us, panting, golden eyes wide and wild, and we'd narrowly miss looping her. Suddenly, she darted into a small inlet that held a garbage dumpster and not much else. The vet ran after her, took aim, and shot. The dart found its mark and the wolf sank to the ground. She lay on her side, the dart protruding from her right flank. Long, silver fur rose and fell heavily with her labored breathing. Her eyes were glazing over. She was quickly losing consciousness. We stood in a circle around her, a majestic, wild animal reduced to lying on the dirty city asphalt, lost and helpless. It was heartbreaking. "We've got to get her back to the East Valley facility," the vet said. The officers carefully lifted the wolf into the truck and we all said our goodbyes. I drove home feeling terribly sad for the captured wolf, worried about the one who was still at large, and more than a little angry at the owner who had put them in this position in the first place.

The next afternoon I got a call from Tia. Raquel, who was known by her neighbors as "the wolf lady" (we all were, it seemed), had received a call that morning from a woman who had been more than a little surprised to find a wolf under her porch. It was, of course, the missing male. Raquel had immediately driven over there and, using treats, a soft voice, and plenty of patience, coaxed the wolf out. Having been somewhat accustomed to people, and probably more than a little hungry, the wolf eventually took treats from Raquel's hand, and she was able to gently loop the rope around his neck. She drove him to the shelter herself. I couldn't help but think how much more easily it could have gone for the poor female the day before, had we been allowed to help.

Both wolves were held at the shelter for a few days as arrangements were made for a nearby wildlife sanctuary to take them. Despite my bronchitis having turned into what would later be diagnosed as walking pneumonia, I drove to the shelter to see them. They had been placed in a pen together. I hoped that offered at least some comfort, but even huddled together, they looked awfully scared and miserable in the midst of all the barking and shelter chaos.

Raquel discovered the identity of the owner of from whose yard the wolves had escaped. The woman never came forward. The shelter wouldn't have returned the wolves to her anyway. Ironically, not only were wolves illegal in the area, but the woman's fencing was only four feet high! It wouldn't have held a large dog for long, never mind a wolf. The sanctuary finally came to pick up the two, and that was the last I heard of them. I can only hope they lived out their lives in well-deserved comfort and peace.

# 24

# Hit by a Flying Wolf

In some parts of the world, a windy day is bad news. People become cranky and irritable, and complain of fatigue, insomnia, or even nausea, chills, or migraines. Crime rates rise, hospital admissions skyrocket, and suicide attempts are more prevalent than usual. What is it about certain winds that can cause these ill effects? Two words: *positive ions.*

Ions—electrically charged groups of atoms—normally have a fairly equal positive and negative charge. Tumbling water, such as waterfalls and showers, creates an atmosphere of negative ions. Researchers have found that negative ions can reduce neurosis and anxiety, heighten thirst, and even stimulate sexual behavior. Positive ions have the opposite effect. (Yes, ladies, you can now say, "Not tonight, dear—too many positive ions.") Generated by dry conditions, positively charged winds are known in Switzerland as the Foehn, in Italy as the Sirocco, in western Canada as the Chinook, and in southern California, as the Santa Anas. The accompanying ill effects may explain why Phantom hates the wind so much.

Because our mini-ranch is nestled among gently sloping mountains at the end of a long canyon road, air currents are buffeted to and fro, picking up force as they go. At certain times of the year, it's not unusual for winds to whip up to near-hurricane force. The wolves, being sensitive creatures, often became agitated when the Santa Anas blew. They paced back and forth nervously, muzzles raised, sniffing the air for danger and sometimes whining. I wished I could protect them from anything that scared them. I constantly worried about them down there in the enclosure. It was like having a part of my heart living outside of my body. And so, one day when the Santa Anas began to howl, I hurried down the steps to make sure the wolves weren't too stressed out.

Sequoia and Heyoka seemed to be okay, although they were pacing a bit. Phantom seemed much more nervous than usual. With my ever-present Mom Instinct at work, I decided to enter the enclosure and try to comfort him. I carefully closed the chain link gate behind me and walked over to one of the wooden tables that C.C. and I had built. There were three: a five-foot-high center table with solid block legs and a piece of plywood for a surface, and a three-foot-high version on either side of it. The wolves delighted in chasing each other around, jumping playfully from one table up to the next and then down the other side. I'd often climb up to the high middle table, get Phantom's attention, and then pat the space next to me. In a flash of black fur, he would appear beside me. I'd scritch-scratch his body from head to tail as he walked back and forth like a contented cat, all but purring. At times, he would even roll over on his back for a tummy rub. Now, that was an event! Long, gangly limbs flailing in the air, he'd squirm with pleasure. There was no question that Phantom was in wolf heaven. As much as I also enjoyed those sessions, I was always afraid he was going to squirm right off the table. Fortunately, it never happened. At the end of those visits, Phantom would contentedly jump down to the lower table, then to the ground, and go about his business.

On this extra-windy day, I sat on one of the lower tables with my back propped up against the high one. Phantom, perhaps out of habit, sprang onto the lower table and then continued past me on to the higher one behind me. As the wind blew its spooky sonata through the chain link, I could feel the tension coming off Phantom in waves. I was looking at the other wolves, thinking again how I wished I could protect them from things that frightened them, when my head was suddenly snapped forward with incredible force. Phantom had, for the first time ever, leaped off the top table without even attempting to touch the lower one. The power of the blow was incredible. It felt as though someone had struck me in the back of the head with a lead pipe—a 140-pound lead pipe, that is. Even in my state of shock, I knew I had to leave the pen immediately. As much as the wolves and I loved and trusted each other, it wouldn't do for me to faint while locked in with them—and I thought I might. I climbed down and made my way unsteadily to the gate.

Outside the enclosure, I hung on to the perimeter fence as dizziness, nausea, disorientation, and pain hit me all at once. I fell to my knees. Trying to look back at the wolves, I found that I couldn't turn my head to either side. This was serious. I was more than a little bit frightened. I made my way slowly back up the stairs, leaning heavily on the arm rail for support. Those 38 steps seemed like 300. Finally, I managed to get into the house, and called C.C. at work. An hour later we sat waiting in the emergency room of the local hospital. I was still dizzy and in pain, but managed to fill out the required intake forms. When I got to the question about what type of accident I'd had, I hesitated. What should I write? *Hit by a flying wolf?* They'd send me to the psych ward for sure. I settled on "whiplash" and figured I could come up with a plausible story by the time the doctor showed up for the examination.

The doctor who treated me was kind and gentle, and I ended up telling her exactly what had happened. She did look at me a bit strangely as I related how I'd been hit in the head by my poor, frightened wolf. Perhaps she was wondering just how much head trauma I'd suffered. Fortunately, she seemed to accept my explanation. As it turned out, I did have a mild concussion but no permanent physical damage. It would take a while, but my neck would heal.

The incident wasn't funny at the time, but looking back it is...well, if not exactly humourous, then at least unusual. I'm guessing the number of members of the People Who Have Been Hit by a Flying Wolf club is pretty small. Years later, whenever I hear the Santa Anas' mournful howl, I still remember that day.

*25*

# Apocalypse Now

I love that our house is nestled against sage-covered hills. The desert is lovely, and being situated at the end of the long dirt road is a blessing in many ways. Traffic is almost non-existent, and there's very little noise from the neighbors. On the other hand, high, dry brush surrounds us on all sides. It's like living in the middle of a tinderbox. There's only one way out of this canyon, and we're as far from it as you can get. That fact becomes particularly worrisome when the humidity is low, the mercury has risen past the 100-degree mark, and those darned winds kick up. It's the perfect recipe for a wildfire.

June through October is considered "fire season" in southern California. During October and November, when the Santa Anas sweep through the canyons like angry ghosts, the danger increases. October 21, 2007 was the start of our own personal apocalypse. We'd heard on the news that two fires were burning, one on either side of us. The more distant fire was in Castaic, eleven miles north. The closer one was fifteen minutes up the road. Television newscasters kept describing the winds as being "hurricane force." They weren't kidding. We could hear the gusts whipping around the house, lashing at the windows and moaning like a cat in heat. Our grab-it-and-go bags were at the ready as usual. Strangely, while mine consisted of one bag filled with important papers, photographs and one change of wardrobe, C.C.'s seemed to be a full set of luggage. Guess which one of us would be stuck having to borrow clothing if push came to shove.

Mojo was in the house with us, so I wasn't overly worried about him. If we had to evacuate, he would ride in the passenger seat of C.C.'s little Honda del Sol and I'd drive the Jeep, as it could fit a crate in the back. Sequoia had passed on from a rare form of cancer at age thirteen, leaving only Phantom and Heyoka. I had crates in the enclosure that were large enough for each of them but, as I've mentioned, Heyoka had always been incredibly skittish and difficult to wrangle. Although we could provide a life with much more space and personal attention, I knew in my heart that in an emergency, given his arousal levels, it would be virtually impossible to get him contained quickly. It was one of the down sides to having taken him in as an adult without the benefits of early handling and socialization. I had looked into dart guns and other options, but in the end I'd been unable to come up with a viable solution. We did make sure that all of the dry brush was cleared from around the enclosure, though, so a fire wouldn't have any fuel and would therefore be a lot less of a threat.

Phantom, with his fear of the wind, was extremely anxious that day. He and Heyoka paced nervously around and around the perimeter of the enclosure, glancing about as though they expected something to jump out at them. I wasn't doing much better. I paced nervously around the house, looking out of the windows and checking the news on television and online. At least it didn't sound from the reports as though the fires were moving in our direction.

The wind had begun raging so strongly that it was almost deafening, even through the double-paned living room windows. That would explain why, when the police drove up our road shouting through a bullhorn that we needed to evacuate, we never heard a thing. What we did hear a short time later was a frantic knocking at our front door. It was John, our neighbor from across the road. He seemed harried, and we soon learned why: The fire was now on the back side of the hill behind our house! We needed to get out right away. The rest of the neighbors had already left.

My first thought was for the wolves. While C.C. loaded the Jeep, I headed for the enclosure with a bag full of hot dogs. I tried to appear relaxed as I slipped inside the pen. I spoke calmly to Phantom, while tossing one hot dog piece after another on the ground where he could snatch them into his powerful jaws. To say that he was food motivated was an understatement and, fortunately, he wasn't too worried to eat. Our tentative Dance of the Hot Dogs moved gradually closer to the entrance of the catch pen and, finally, inside it. I quickly stepped in after Phantom and closed the gate. Getting him into the crate was another matter. Although I'd made some headway with getting him comfortable entering a crate, it had been extremely difficult to practice when there had been three wolves in the enclosure, and I'd had so much else going on that I hadn't kept it up. There we were, me tossing hot dog pieces into the crate, and Phantom warily stretching his neck forward, sticking his head in only as far as necessary to grab the pieces, and then quickly retreating. As I continued my lame attempts to coax him inside, the fire crested the hill behind our house and began burning down toward us.

C.C. appeared outside the enclosure and shouted in a breathless, worried voice, "Come on, Nicole! We have to go. The Jeep's parked just down the road and I have to run back up the hill to get the car."

"I'm not leaving Phantom here!" I shouted. "Quick, come in here." With an exasperated look, C.C. entered the pen. Heyoka, who had always been flat-out afraid of men, and who was now especially nervous with all that was going on, kept a safe distance. Phantom had always been a little bit frightened of C.C. despite the fact that the nice man tossed him raw chicken every day for breakfast. (What ever happened to classical conditioning?) But no matter. I hoped to use that bit of fear to my advantage.

"Come and stand right outside the catch pen," I urged. As C.C. walked forward, I blocked Phantom's escape route so he had nowhere to go other than into the crate. Phantom glanced at the opening of the crate and looked around for other options. C.C. moved in closer. Phantom looked around frantically, the whites of his eyes showing, and made an attempt to get past me. I stood firm. Finally, he put the front half of his body into the crate—and froze. He was clearly scared of the crate, afraid of C.C., and almost paralyzed by fear. I had no idea how he'd react if I tried to push him further inside. Would he whip around and bite me? I knew an uninhibited bite from a pure wolf, especially a frightened one, would cause major injury. But we were out of time. I sent a quick appeal out to the Powers That Be, grabbed Phantom around the waist, and shoved. A second later I slammed the crate door shut behind him.

Phantom was one of the biggest wolves I've ever known. As I've mentioned, he weighed 140 pounds. The giant-sized Varikennel added another 40 pounds. It must have been the adrenaline rush that allowed C.C. and me to get the crate out of the enclosure and into the road, all the while keeping an eye on the fire that was now eating its way much too quickly through the brush. Already at the bottom of the hill, it was racing toward us. At the top of the hill, another set of flames blazed a trail toward the house. There was nothing we could do. C.C. ran up the driveway and got his car. I opened the hatchback of my Jeep, and when he returned, we loaded the crate into it. Or, I should say, we *tried* to load the crate into it. The crate was one I'd borrowed from Tia months before, and somehow I'd assumed that, like the others, it would fit. I cursed myself for being so stupid. How could I not have tried it? Phantom couldn't fit into a smaller crate, and now we were out of time.

"*Nicole*," C.C. said in a stern tone I'd never heard before, "we have to go." He began to walk quickly away from the Jeep, toward his car.

The crate with Phantom in it was sitting in the middle of the dirt road, and the fire was coming. "I can't just leave Phantom here!" I cried. Surely there was a way to bring him with us. It was bad enough that we had to leave Heyoka. That we couldn't take either of them seemed impossible. Just thinking about it caused my chest to tighten to the point that I thought I might collapse. But I had to focus on the task at hand. Through the smoke and the thick clouds of swirling debris, I could see the look of exasperation on C.C.'s face.

"What are we going to do?" he shouted over the wind.
I knew he was right. It was extremely dangerous for us to stay where we were. Tears streamed down my face. I felt completely helpless. How could I leave the wolves behind? How could I have been so stupid about the crate? There had to be some other answer. I'd always known that we couldn't evacuate Heyoka. But I couldn't leave Phantom, too. I just couldn't.

Just then, like an angel, our neighbor John materialized. Through the dust storm, I could make out his white open-bed pickup truck coming up the road. I saw that it had exactly enough room left in back to carry a large crate with one very nervous wolf in it. What were the chances? Sobbing with relief, I flagged him down. He and C.C. quickly loaded the crate into the truck. "Head over to the VFW," John shouted over the wind. We all jumped in our vehicles and tore off down the dirt road, away from the fast-approaching flames.

When we reached the paved main road, we could see flames licking down the mountains on both sides of us. The wind howled. Dust was everywhere, like a sepia filter laid over the landscape. We followed John down Sierra Highway and into the dirt lot of the VFW (Veterans of Foreign Wars) hall and parked next to him. I immediately ran over to check on Phantom. He was a mass of black, quivering fur, cowering as far back into the crate as he could. Squinting through the dust, I tried to block the wind and soothe him, but it wasn't having any visible effect. A few of the people who hurried by asked, "Whose wolf?" As I hadn't planned for this to be a coming-out party for Phantom, I ignored them and draped a towel as best I could over the front of the crate.

Inside the small, rustic meeting hall that served as a bar and gathering place for the VFW, a table set against the back wall held boxes of pizza, soft drinks, and other emergency rations. Some of our neighbors, John included, frequented the place regularly, and they now sat around the bar discussing the fire. The large plasma television screens that lined the walls all held the same horrific images. It was surreal. We could watch the coverage on television, and then, by sticking our heads out the back door, see the exact same fiery scenes. We took a seat at the bar. People drank and ate, and drank some more. We all remained glued to the televisions, waiting to see whether our houses were burning. More than a few kind folks urged me to eat something, but I was so sick at the thought of Heyoka being stuck in the enclosure that it was all I could do not to vomit or hyperventilate. I also had a searing pain in my left shoulder, which I'd later find out was due to having torn my rotator cuff when we'd tried to lift Phantom's crate into the Jeep. But pain was the least of my worries.

I kept imagining the worst. I knew the flames couldn't burn into the pen, but I did think it was possible that Heyoka could be overcome by smoke. I honestly didn't know whether we'd find him alive when we returned. When I confessed my worries to a man seated next to me at the bar, he asked why we hadn't just set Heyoka free. While that might seem logical, the truth was that we would have had almost no chance of ever getting him back. At the sanctuary where he'd lived almost his entire life, he hadn't needed to do anything to earn his food, unless you counted lying there looking cute. In the wild, he would most likely starve to death slowly.

Sometime after covering Phantom's crate, before entering the bar, I'd phoned Tia. She had driven down immediately. When she arrived, all I could do was jabber hysterically over and over, "Heyoka! I couldn't get him out!" Although the police and fire department had assured us that no one would be allowed to pass through the main roads, Tia knew a back route. With her two helpers, she made a valiant attempt to wind her way back through the dangerous roads to rescue Heyoka. C.C. followed them, leaving me to keep an eye on Phantom in the crate and Mojo in the Jeep. I knew if anyone could corner a frightened wolf and get him into a crate, it was Tia. I cried, and waited, and cried some more. Eventually, they returned. They'd gotten more than halfway to the house, only to be turned away by the police. My heart sank. I took some solace in the fact that we'd gotten Phantom out. We transferred his crate to Tia's van, and she drove off into the glowing orange landscape with Phantom in tow. He would spend the night crated in her van. At least he was safe for now.

For the next two hours, we checked on Mojo, watched the news reports, and waited. The news was not good. The Buckweed Fire, as they had dubbed it, was not at all contained. The wind continued to rage, which caused the fire to spread at an alarming rate. Structures were threatened and some were already burning, although it was hard to tell from the reports exactly where they were located. Strangely, up until that moment, I hadn't spared a thought for our house. Of course, it would be terrible if we lost it, along with all of our belongings. But Heyoka's safety was foremost in my mind.

My friend Leslie lived in the San Fernando Valley, and she'd offered us shelter for the night. She lived in a guesthouse behind a lovely middle-aged couple who were dog lovers. They had an empty kennel run, and had told Leslie we were welcome to board Mojo there overnight. After sitting in the bar for another hour with no change in the news, it was almost midnight. We decided to take Leslie up on her offer. We headed out into the smoke-filled streets.

The scene on the roads was unreal. It was a fiery apocalypse. Mountains of flames surrounded us on both sides and shot sparks up into the sky. The smoke and dust were so thick that we could barely make out the white lines separating the lanes. Finally, we made it to the freeway. As the miles passed, as worried as I was about Heyoka, it was a relief to leave the horrific scene behind and to fill our lungs with clean air.

We arrived at Leslie's house at 2:00 a.m., red-eyed and reeking of smoke. We got Mojo situated in the kennel and grabbed a change of clothing from our bags. After filling Leslie in on the events of the night and confirming online that there were no further developments, we all went to sleep. Or, I should say, Leslie retired to her room and C.C. fell asleep on the sofabed she'd made up for us. I couldn't sleep. The minutes ticked by painfully slowly as vision after unpleasant vision replayed on the insides of my eyelids: The fire moving relentlessly down the hill toward us. Standing in the middle of the road with Phantom in the crate, feeling helpless. Heyoka stuck in the enclosure. Heyoka. I tried to cry quietly so as not to wake C.C. What kind of rescue person was I, leaving Heyoka there? How could I ever live with myself if something happened to him? Even as I tried to reassure myself that everything would be fine, I couldn't help but beat myself up over it.

I never did fall asleep. But, despite my endless procession of worrisome visions, the sun still rose. Once C.C. was awake, I turned on the television. The fires were still burning out of control. More homes had been destroyed. Our neighbor John had given me his cell phone number before we'd left him at the VFW lodge, and had said we could call anytime to check in. He also knew the back roads, and had been planning to sneak back to his house, despite the official warning to stay away until the all clear was sounded. It was 6:00 a.m. when I called, and John had obviously been asleep. I quickly apologized, and asked what was happening.

"Oh man," he said groggily, "the firefighters totally saved your house. They were in your driveway from midnight until 4:30 in the morning."

"Heyoka? How is Heyoka? You know, the wolf in the pen."

"Don't worry," John said, "He's fine." I exhaled a sigh of relief.

He continued, "There were four women firefighters. I've never seen a crew of all women before. They were all really concerned that he had enough water and that he was okay. They kept checking on him. Really, he's just fine, and so is your house. I think you're safe to come on back." It was as though a hand that had been squeezing my heart since the previous day finally eased up. I relayed the message to C.C., and we reported the good news to Leslie when she awoke. After feeding Mojo, grabbing a quick breakfast, and thanking Leslie profusely for the emergency hospitality, we headed home.

~ * ~ * ~ * ~ * ~ * ~ * ~ *

There had been multiple, huge, out of control fires burning in Los Angeles all at the same time, and firefighters had been spread thin. By the time the largest one—the Station Fire—was fully contained on October 16th over 160,000 acres had burned and 209 structures were destroyed, including

89 homes. Two firefighters had died trying to escape the flames when their truck plunged off a cliff. It was the largest wildfire in the modern history of Los Angeles County, and it was later discovered to be the result of arson. The Buckweed Fire, which turned out to have been started by a ten-year-old boy playing with matches, burned over 38,000 acres. Considering the tragic scope of the fires, we'd been very lucky. That the house had been saved was amazing, but mainly I was just grateful that we were all okay.

We are still vigilant about keeping the brush cut way back from all structures. But every time the temperature soars into the 100s and the winds gust, I can't help but think of the fiery apocalypse of that terrible day. On edge, I watch and wait.

26

# Scorpions, Tarantulas, and Rattlesnakes—Oh, My!

Growing up in Brooklyn, New York was far different from living with wolves in the desert in every possible way. My experiences with wildlife were limited to being startled by the cockroaches that would scurry out of the kitchen sink when I turned on the lights to grab a midnight snack, and spying the large rats who lived around the subway tracks throughout the city. You would think those encounters might have in some way prepared me to deal with startling critters, but I was in no way ready for southern California's Creatures of the Desert.

To be fair, not all of our desert wildlife is frightening. There are finger-sized, pale green lizards that lounge on the river rocks in front of the house and cling to the stucco porch walls waiting for unsuspecting insects to fly by. Birds perch in the plentiful pepper trees, bathe in puddles left by the sprinklers, and occasionally build nests on the flat wooden top of the wind chimes that hang outside our front door. Birdsong is often the sole soundtrack in this serene canyon.

We share the hillsides with a large population of grey, long-eared desert cottontail rabbits. Their large brown eyes, long ears, and white puffy tails make them look almost artificially cute, like little stuffed animals. They love the prickly produce that grows on the sprawling mega-cactus that spans the front of the house. Each year when Godzilla, as C.C. dubbed it, produces plum-like fruits, C.C. carefully plucks them with a pair of giant metal tongs and rolls them along the ground to the eagerly awaiting bunny congregation. Every night when he gets home from work they're out there waiting, all but thumping their paws and saying, "It's about time!" They have him well trained.

I've learned a few things over the years as a spectator at the Bunny Fruit Bowl. For one thing, those oh-so-cute cottontails can get downright nasty over things they consider valuable. They'll hop straight up in the air in a demonstration of bunny bravado, aiming to run each other off a piece of fruit. Sharing happens, but it is short-lived. And there is definitely something special in that fruit…something that gets rabbits *drunk*. Okay, maybe bunny inebriation isn't exactly what's happening, but it sure seems like it. Whiskers aquiver, the bunnies gnaw at the rough skin of the fruit to release the sweet, pulpy innards. Once they've taken their fill, they wobble around like little furry drunkards, scrubbing with dainty paws at the incriminating dark red stains that encircle their mouths. But as much as they love the fruit, they constantly keep their large radar dish ears tuned to the local predator station, Coyote FM, which I'm sure plays a round-the-clock version of the old Iron Maiden song, "Run to the Hills."

One of the first things we did when we bought our property, other than building the wolf enclosure, was to install chain link along the back side of the house to create a large dog run. The fencing was meant to not only keep the dogs in, but to keep wildlife out. Our wild neighbors include plenty of the aforementioned coyotes, and also the occasional bobcat. The coyotes lope confidently down the hillside and sometimes stand right at the fence line, staring at the house. This was a problem when Mojo was alive, as he would step through the dog door and spy a coyote on *his* property. He'd rush out of the house, all hackles and snarls, rear up on his hind legs, and bark furiously at the offender. More often than not, the coyote would just stand there staring as though Mojo had lost his mind.

As Mojo got older, all that frantic jumping became harder on his hips, so I'd try to convince the coyotes to leave before he spotted them. My attempts at banishment were effective at times, and at others…not so much. I would walk boldly up to the fence and in a firm voice command, "Go home!" The proclamation was accompanied by an authoritative wave of the arm. Sometimes it actually worked. At other times I fared no better than Mojo. The coyote would stand there staring, clearly unimpressed. I could almost see the thought bubble over his head: *I* am *home. Who are you?* He had a point.

Coyotes have a high-pitched, blood-curdling, banshee yip of a howl that is completely different than the low, mournful tones produced by wolves.

The high-pitched chorus of *yaayaayaaay* makes it sound as though there are at least ten wild savages in the nearby hills, tearing something cute and furry to shreds. In the dead of the night, it's chilling. But I learned something interesting on a recent trip to Wolf Park, a wolf research and education center in Indiana. Our private tour took us past a pair of captive coyotes. When I mentioned those sounds I'd hear in the mountains at night and asked whether coyotes hunted in packs, the staff member coaxed the resident duo to howl. Although there were clearly only two coyotes standing in front of us, the sound resonated like a chorus. While the sound can still raises *my* hackles on dark desert nights, it's comforting to know there are probably fewer gangs of marauding coyotes out there than I suspected.

Although their howls can be chilling, I have a definite fondness for the coyotes. They're beautiful, efficient predators who can stand their ground or be gone in the blink of an eye. The bobcats, too, are exotic, graceful creatures that fascinate me and always prompt me to run for my camera. My fondness for the desert creatures, however, does not extend to the scorpions, toward which I cannot find it in my heart to feel warm and fuzzy. The first time I spied one, it was lounging in my bathtub. Fortunately for me, I was not in the tub at the time. Fortunately for the scorpion, neither was the water. I normally scoop spiders and other insects into a jar and deposit them outside, sending them on their merry way. But not having any idea of how a scorpion might react to an attempt at capture— can they jump, and if so, how high and how fast?—I woke C.C. and asked him to please escort Mr. Stingy-tail to the great outdoors. Then I went online to research scorpions. I can now safely say that I feel mighty fortunate to have encountered only the small yellow variety. If I ever see one that resembles the large, black, sci-fi creatures I saw on those websites, you'll hear my screams.

We've had nine scorpions in the house in the ten years we've lived here. Although it's always startling to happen upon one, we've pretty much gotten used to them. You'd think the scorpions and maybe a couple of bees or moths would be the only creepy crawlies that would make it inside the house, but *noooo*. One night, I was lying on the couch watching television. I was half-dozing when something scurried along the baseboard of the far wall. I jerked upright and squinted into the dim light, unable to make out what it was. As I stood up, I asked C.C. to get the bug jar. While he was in the kitchen, I crept closer to get a better look. "Uh, honey? You're gonna need a bigger jar," I called, feeling like Roy Scheider in *Jaws*. The tarantula was black, hairy, and roughly the size of my fist. Trust me, there's nothing fitting that description you'd want crawling around your house. Fortunately, my knight in shining nightshirt got the tarantula safely into the jar and outside.

As disconcerting as they might be, none of the aforementioned creepy-crawlies is as flat-out frightening—or as dangerous—as that king of scary desert creatures, the rattlesnake. I've learned over the years to be at least somewhat comfortable with a variety of snakes. I have no quarrel with the non-poisonous ones, as long as we stick to our unwritten agreement to ignore each other unless I'm taking photographs. Besides, King snakes actually keep the rodent population down and keep the more dangerous snakes away, and they're more than welcome to set up camp under the house any time they like. King snakes, gopher snakes, fine. But *rattlesnakes*? They completely freak this Brooklyn girl out, and dealing with them is most definitely not in my frame of reference. But as it turns out, thanks to Phantom, that's exactly what I had to do.

A few summers ago, C.C. found a rattlesnake in back of the house. It was on the dirt hill just beyond the chain link fence. It was dead. The diamond-patterned skin had been sliced open, the snake having committed a reptile version of hari-kari by slithering through the sharp wire of the garden fencing that surrounded an ill-fated attempt by the previous owners to grow veggies. Naturally, my first thought was that the snake could have easily gotten through the chain link and bitten our dogs, who might not know to leave a dangerous snake alone. I went searching on the internet and discovered something called snake tongs. Yes, there really is such a product, created expressly to pick up creepy, crawly snakes in a way that helps soft, puncture-prone humans to feel a whole lot safer. Not only that, but there's a "bagger system" to put the snake in once it's been captured. I bought both, because really, what's the point of being all tonged up with nowhere to go?

The tongs consisted of a blue, three-foot-long aluminum pole with a thick metal grip at one end. When squeezed, the grip caused the metal tongs to close like a pair of steely jaws. The bagger system turned out to be not so much of a "system" as a long, narrow burlap sack within another sack that hung from the end of a metal pole. The bag's smallish triangular opening was kept rigid by metal tubing. Although I felt somewhat better once the set arrived, I had a hard time imagining myself actually using it. As though even handling the apparatus might conjure up a rattlesnake, I stashed it in the back of the broom closet and promptly forgot all about it.

A year later, on a blazing hot midsummer day, I went down to the wolf enclosure to visit with Phantom. Heyoka had passed away that February, leaving Phantom alone. Because of Phantom's temperament—let's call it "discerning"—we hadn't been able to safely pair him with another wolf from the rescue center. Because he was by himself, I'd been spending more time with him, spoiling him silly with all manner of treats, petting, and tummy rubs. He would hear my footsteps on the wooden stairway and jump with excitement, and then, anticipating attention, run up and jam his big muzzle between the chain link gate and the post. But today he was nowhere near the gate. As I neared the bottom step, I could see him pacing in a large, nervous arc around the back of the pen. "What's gotten into you, buddy?" I called. "Come on, I'm your last friend," I coaxed, as I crouched to unclip the chain from the gate.

The entrance gate was made of heavy chain link like the rest of the enclosure, but we'd also wired a plywood board to it after one of the wolves had chewed through a weakened portion of the chain link. That explains why I couldn't see a thing as I crouched and stuck my hand between the gate and the post to unclip the bottom chain. I fumbled with it a bit, and got the clip undone. I stood and unlocked the padlock, flipped the latch, and opened the gate. And stopped breathing. There at my feet, just inside the gate *where I'd just stuck my hand*, was a brown and tan, angular-headed snake with jointed rattles for a tail. Although I'd only seen them in photographs, there was no mistaking the rattlesnake.

The snake was coiled, though not as if to strike. In fact, it seemed to be enjoying the summer heat. That made one of us. I took a careful step back and quietly closed the gate. I extended my arm with my palm toward Phantom as if to say, "Stay back!" He looked at me with a frantic gaze that could only be translated as, *Do I look like I'm going anywhere near that thing?* I glanced over at the metal poop scooper. Could it double as a snake scooper? A vision of the snake rearing up from the metal tray did not inspire confidence. Then I remembered the tongs. Running breathlessly up the steps to the house, heart pounding much too fast, I located the tongs and bag. I had just whirled back around toward the front door when it occurred to me that I'd never actually used the set, and had no idea what I was doing. But a deadly snake was in the enclosure with my wolf! Mojo's large black rubber Kong was lying in the middle of the foyer, so I tried using the tongs to pick it up. Tongs, meet Kong. There, that wasn't so hard. I rushed back downstairs, armed and ready to defend my boy.

Phantom was still doing the *Mom, keep that scary thing away from me!* dance. With the tongs in one hand and the bag-on-a-pole in the other, I quietly opened the gate. The rattlesnake was in the same position I'd left it. Good. I said a quick, silent prayer, then extended the pole toward the snake. With a calm, decisive motion, I clamped the tongs around the sleek, scaly neck. A moment later I lifted the thick body, all five feet of it, into the air. It was *heavy*. The photo on the website had depicted a docile snake being placed easily into a burlap sack. This snake was not only heavy, but it was no longer calm. In fact, it seemed downright annoyed at having its afternoon nap interrupted. The last foot of the body curled and thrashed, and I got a good look at those infamous rattles. There looked to be at least six or seven of them, but getting a precise count was not foremost on my mind. The thrashing made it difficult to keep the tail centered over the narrow opening of the bag, and that rattling sound, well, rattled me! Finally, I got the rattles in position, lowered the body into the bag, and released the jaws of the tongs. Somehow I'd assumed the bag apparatus had a pressure closure similar to a mop wringer, but there were only strings which, at the moment, looked awfully flimsy. I knotted them together and then knotted them twice more for good measure. Who knew what Houdini-like skills a wily rattler might possess?

I latched the gate to the pen and breathed a sigh of relief. I'm sure Phantom did, too. All was well…except that I was now holding a rattlesnake in a bag on a stick. What did one do in this situation? Was there some protocol? I scoured my memory and came up blank. I climbed carefully back up the stairs, holding the heavy bag away from my body. At the back of the house I spied our large plastic recycling bin. Ah! That looked like a good option. I flipped open the lid and found the bin empty inside, save for a bed of leaves. I nervously dropped the bag in, pole and all. I then closed the lid and resumed breathing. I placed a large cement paver stone on top of the lid, just in case.

So now I had a rattlesnake in a bag on a pole in a bin. It was progress, but I still wanted the snake *gone*. A quick online search yielded the website of a local man who was a snake whisperer of sorts. If residents found a rattlesnake on their property and were willing to capture it rather than kill it, Hugo would drive out and take the snake off their hands. Not only that, but he'd take it home, make sure it was well hydrated and happy, and then release it back into an unpopulated wilderness area. I had visions of a serpentine Club Med where slithery guests received soothing massages as snake-charming music played in the background. Snapping out of it, I called Hugo and arranged for him to come over as soon as possible. Then I called C.C. at work to tell him about what had happened. His end of the conversation consisted of a lot of, "You did *what?*"

Less than thirty minutes later, a white van appeared in the driveway. A pleasantly weathered, forty-something man hopped out and introduced himself as Hugo. When he asked where the snake was, I pointed at the recycling bin across the driveway, unwilling to move any closer. As much as I'd kept myself together while capturing the snake, by now I was shaky. As Hugo slid the van door open, he explained that he was a middle-school teacher who had always loved snakes. In fact, he bred and rescued them. He had over 300 snakes in his garage and, apparently, one very understanding wife. When he brought out a small plastic container with an airtight spin top, I looked at it dubiously. In a reprise of my Roy Scheider imitation, I said, "I think you're going to need a bigger container."

Just then, C.C. drove up. As we stood in the driveway watching, Hugo removed the brick from the top of the recycling bin. He lifted the bag out by the pole and quickly untied my clumsy knots. I expected him to carefully position the bag and, with great finesse, allow the snake to slide safely down into the container, which would be immediately sealed. Instead, he dumped the snake out onto the asphalt. Did this man not comprehend the mental state of a person who would tie knot after knot and then put a brick on top of a bin for extra assurance? Part of my mind tried to register why he'd released the rattlesnake, while another part suggested helpfully, *Run away!*

Instead of wrangling the snake, or at the very least whispering to it, Hugo began to give us an impromptu lecture about snakes. As we stood in a large, loose triangle around the snake, Hugo discussed the rattlesnake's natural

habitat, explained that they weren't naturally aggressive, and…"Uh…
Hugo? Should we be concerned about standing this close?" I interrupted.
We were each roughly four feet from the snake, which, although calm,
wasn't entirely motionless. "Couldn't it strike us?" No, Hugo clarified, a
snake's striking distance is half the length of its body. Somehow the math
did not reassure me. Finally, he picked up a pole with a metal hook at the
end and looped it under the snake. At least that seemed to be the idea.
The first attempt failed, and I took a quick step backward. "Don't worry,"
he said, all crinkly smiles and confidence. The second try was successful,
and he lowered the rattler into the bin. It wasn't until he'd screwed the
top on tight that I realized I'd been holding my breath again.

"Just give a shout if you need me," Hugo called cheerily over his shoulder
as he climbed into his van. As it turned out we did call him again, eight or
nine times over the next six years. We caught more rattlesnakes and even
one Mojave Green, which holds the title for the most dangerous species
of rattlesnake in the United States. Because really, if you're going to tong
a dangerous snake, why not go for the gold? Since none of the snakes
had been threatening the dogs or wolves, and C.C. had been at home
when they'd appeared, I allowed him the honor of tonging and bagging
them. It's good to know, though, that if push comes to shove, this former
Brooklyn girl can wrangle a rattlesnake and keep her canine kids safe.

# 27

# Living with Wolves

People always want to know what it's like to live with wolves. Allow me to illustrate with an example from our everyday lives: One day C.C. walked into the house after work. His nose crinkled, and he asked what was cooking. Standing over a bubbling pot on the stove, I answered, "Cow heart." The way he looked at me said he was thinking I'd be cooking up some eye of newt for dessert.

Cow heart wasn't even the worst of it. I also fed tripe, which is also offal (internal organs). The smell was…well, awful! The scent is right up there with dogs releasing their anal glands. On a yummier and less stinky note, the wolves also got a little bit of yogurt here and there and, twice a week, eggs. I still remember the first time I gave Phantom a raw egg. I had been standing outside the chain link fence with three eggs in a basket. He was so anxious for one that I slipped his through an opening in the chain link. With his usual oh so genteel manner, he clamped his jaws down hard. Milky whites and yellow bits of yolk splattered everywhere! I couldn't help but laugh at poor Phantom, who looked more than a little bit surprised. He was the literal embodiment of the expression "egg on your face." At least it was one trial learning, and he took eggs more gently after that.

As I've mentioned, chicken backs were the staple of the wolves' diet. We rotated them with turkey necks as the main meat source, and supplemented with other items. There were mashed up veggies, and the ever-popular organ meats. I was determined to feed a raw diet properly. With three lupine mouths to feed (not to mention the two dogs), that became expensive. And so I joined a raw food co-op, where the purchasing power of the group kept prices down. Once a month, C.C. and I would drive to a pickup point in the San Fernando Valley. We'd locate the boxes with our name on them, load them up, and drive home. There were boxes of chicken backs, turkey necks, organ meats, and sometimes fish. Phantom, Heyoka, and Sequoia all seemed to like the chunks of fish, as well as the canned sardines I'd buy at the store. One day I got the idea to try giving them whole fish instead. I figured, they're *wolves*, right? Surely they'd tear into a whole fish with glee. I walked into the pen and tossed a whole fish to each of them. Of the three, only Sequoia tore into the fish. The boys just stood there looking puzzled, pawing and sniffing at the weird-looking thing that should have been moving in water.

Something that was a hit with all three, though, was Frosty Paws. Sequoia would lick at the ice cream-like contents of the little paper cup in a dainty, lady-like manner. Heyoka would look at his for about half a second and then dig in. Phantom, however, always had to scent-roll on his before eating it. He would release the cup from his jaws so it landed face up on the pea gravel. He'd sniff it, and then turn his head to the side and lower his neck. His body would follow, turning until he ended up completely on his back. Then he'd squirm back and forth, gangly arms and legs flailing in the air as he ground his fur into the sweet treat. It was one of the funniest things I've ever seen.

In addition to ensuring that the wolves got diversity in their diet, it was important to provide them with a variety of experiences. Unfortunately, we couldn't walk them outside of the enclosure. To me, this was one of the most difficult things to accept. Wolves are illegal where we live, and although Animal Control knew me as part of the rescue center and unofficially knew they were there, part of the deal was that they would be securely contained and never be taken out. They did get exercise by running and playing in the pen, of course. What I couldn't give them with outside stimulation, I tried to make up for with environmental enrichment. We had built the series of plywood tables for them to jump on, and there was a giant wooden spool from the electrical company that served as part of a jungle gym as well. In the summers when it got hot, we brought in a giant plastic tub and filled it with water. Sequoia enjoyed lying in it. Heyoka only sniffed at the water and walked away. Phantom, however, would jump in with all four paws and then splash and paw until all of the water was gone. It was pretty much what I'd expected. At least they seemed to enjoy it.

One day, in the interest of introducing something new and different, we brought in some straw bales. I knew the straw would end up making a mess, but that was okay. I told C.C. as we loaded the bales in, "Sequoia will lie on top of the pile like the queen she is. Heyoka will pee on them, and Phantom will tear them to shreds." Within moments of stacking the bales, that's exactly what happened.

With our dogs, I'd always been able to provide mental stimulation in the form of stuffed Kongs and other food-dispensing toys. But finding things the wolves couldn't shred was a challenge. Even the black Kongs—the toughest ones—couldn't stand up to their strong jaws. I finally discovered the Jolly Ball, a bowling ball-sized sphere made of extremely hard plastic. Into each of three balls I drilled three holes big enough for pieces of kibble or treats to get through. Stuffing them took a while. For the trial run, I used high-quality, salmon-flavored kibble I'd gotten as a sample from a local pet store. It was a hit! The wolves delighted in rolling the balls around and gobbling up whatever fell out. Over time, I rotated the treats to keep it interesting. The wolves never fought over the balls, and the activity certainly kept them busy. It was a beautiful thing.

Not everything was so successful or easy, though. There was the matter of medical care. Even though the vet who treated all the wolves from the rescue center was willing to treat them, getting them there was difficult; you've already heard about the ordeal with Heyoka. I couldn't find a vet willing to come out and see them, either. Even minor physical ailments could present a challenge. Giving pills wasn't so bad, since I could stuff them into hot dogs that the wolves would, well, wolf down. But one summer we had a huge problem with flies. No matter how careful I was about keeping the enclosure feces-free, the flies had apparently chosen the area as their summer hangout. Sequoia didn't seem that bothered, but Phantom's ears started to show fly bites, and Heyoka's ears got the worst of it. I knew it would be difficult to get the thick, pink fly repellent ointment on to Phantom's ears, and almost impossible to get it on Heyoka's. If the wolves even saw me walk in with the container, they would immediately become suspicious.

At first, I concealed the small jar in my bra under my T-shirt and walked into the pen as I normally would. I sat on the ground calmly stroking Phantom on his face and down his side. Once he gave the deep sigh that told me he was becoming relaxed, I surreptitiously got some of the ointment onto my fingers, and stroked some on his ears. Of course, after the first touch he knew something was up, and after the second, he was on his feet; but at least it had worked. As for Heyoka, since I couldn't pet him at all, I had to get creative. There was a large log we'd brought in as part of our ongoing enrichment program. I'd periodically spray or spread different scents on it for the wolves to investigate and scent roll on. I slathered the log in two different places with the thick, pink ointment. Lo and behold, scent rolling ensued! The ointment reached its target of the wolves' ears…and then their faces, and their bodies. Although I assured them that they still looked like the regal wolves that they were, they did look awfully silly peppered with pink polka dots.

Another thing I had to get creative about was controlling their howling. I didn't expect that they would never howl. In fact, it was one of my greatest joys to drive up the hill to our house and hear a melodious welcome home chorus. Sequoia would start it off and the boys would join in, always managing to create beautiful harmonies. But the soulful sonata didn't only happen when I came home. The wolves would howl at sirens, or in answer to coyotes in the hills behind our house. It wasn't troublesome during the day, but it was definitely a problem at four in the morning. The last thing I wanted was for our neighbors to call Animal Control.

The enclosure was down the hill a ways from the house, and yelling "Quiet!" just wasn't going to cut it. I purchased a high-quality ultrasonic kennel silencer that would, when triggered by sound, emit a piercing beep that only the wolves could hear. It worked for a while, and then the box got damaged in an especially bad rainstorm. I had to come up with something until the replacement arrived. I remembered that when the wolves first came to live with us, they were frightened whenever C.C. used the leaf blower. He'd stopped using it, and it had been sitting in the storage shed for months. I had an idea. I ran it by C.C., who agreed to help, although he looked almost as dubious as when he found me boiling a heart on the stove.

We suspended the leaf blower by a strong chain right outside the wolf pen, and then ran a very long extension cord up the hill to the house. The cord entered our bedroom by way of a small hole cut into the window screen, and plugged into a power strip on the floor by my side of the bed. When the button on the power strip was pushed, the leaf blower would roar into life. Those first few nights I slept even more lightly than usual, just waiting for the wolves to howl. Naturally, they didn't. But on the fourth night, I heard Heyoka howling, Sequoia joining in, and then Phantom's low, mournful howl. I pressed the button. The blower let out a loud, whirring rumble. The howling stopped immediately. I was quite pleased with myself—for a week, anyway. That's how long it took for the wolves to acclimate to the sound and begin to ignore it. Fortunately, the replacement kennel silencer arrived not long after.

In other areas, I had more success. I had done extensive handling work with Phantom, and we were making progress with crate training. There was a behavior, though, that still needed to be addressed: Phantom practically body tackled me whenever I entered the enclosure to feed them. I would walk in with a bucket of chicken backs, and Sequoia and Heyoka would hang back, waiting for me to toss pieces to them. Phantom, however, had no self-control. I wouldn't even have time to latch the gate behind me before he rushed over and dive bombed me, forcefully shoving his head into the bucket, practically knocking me backward in the process. This was definitely not okay. I had to teach him to back up. I'd taught dogs to back up by placing them between a couch and a coffee table, effectively creating a narrow corridor, and then walking into their space. In the enclosure I didn't have that luxury. But I knew Phantom would be a bit frightened if I raised my arms, and so I began to walk in and then raise both arms in the air, one holding the bucket, and the other flicking a wrist forward as I moved into Phantom's space, saying, "Back! Back! Back!" It worked. Soon I could say the words without having to raise my arms and he would back up. I still gave Phantom his chicken first, but I was able to establish a routine where each wolf got fed in a separate corner of the pen, which helped to keep the peace.

Food was important to all three of them, of course, but of even higher value were the marrow bones—raw cow femurs—they got twice weekly. The wolves absolutely loved them. As far as chew items, the femurs were the only things that would last longer than fifteen minutes. Although there were never fights over the bones, Sequoia definitely had an opinion about people being near her when she was in possession of one. This opinion could be summed up in one word: "Mine!" Although I would never have tried to take a bone away from any of them (why teach them

that bad things happen when people come near their stuff?), I did need
to be safe in the pen while Sequoia had a bone. It wouldn't do for me to
be scooping poop and inadvertently come too close and get bitten. With
a dog, I would have implemented a behavior modification protocol for
resource guarding. But again, everything was different with the wolves.
In the end, I decided to simply let Sequoia learn over time that I was no
threat, that I would never even *think* of taking her bone. I began to spend
time just sitting at a distance that she seemed comfortable with while
she chewed. She was wary at first, keeping one eye on me and one on the
bone, but over time she learned to trust me. In the end, I could sit right
next to her, stroking the fur down her back as she happily chomped away.

As anyone who's read my books on wolfdogs knows, I don't recommend
that people run out and get pet wolves. Mine came to me because of
unfortunate situations that had already been created, and I did the best
for them that I could. I always felt that Sequoia and Phantom were pretty
happy with their lot here. But my heart always hurt for Heyoka, who was
an old, sensitive soul. He was the epitome of the wise "alpha." With the
merest curl of his lip and a meaningful look, he could get Phantom to roll
over on his back and submit. Heyoka had a quiet, thoughtful air and a still,
powerful energy. No matter how well I treated the three, and no matter
how much good food, mental stimulation, and affection I could offer, I
felt he was resigned to his lot. Sure, he played, experienced enjoyment,
and had the companionship of the other wolves and me. But of the three,
it just seemed so *wrong* for him to be anywhere other than running free.
At least we had our special moments, and I was always happy to give
affection on his terms.

Sequoia's only complaint was not getting petted enough. On freezing cold
winter days, I would walk down the steps to the enclosure. Halfway down,
I'd see her spinning in circles and hear her excited, "Roo! Roo!" I began
to call her my Little Roo Girl. I would enter the enclosure and she'd run
up to me with her tail wagging wildly. I'd crouch down and she would
rush into my arms and place her head over my shoulder. With my arms
around her, we'd both enjoy a heartfelt cuddle. Many canines, whether
dog or wolf, don't like to be hugged—but Sequoia absolutely loved it.

Something *I* really loved was spending time every day with all three of my
wolfy fur-kids. There is just something utterly unique about the energy of

wolves. I was once interviewed for the National Public Radio show *All Things Considered*, and was asked about the differences between spending time with dogs and wolves. Part of my answer was that a dog's energy is somewhat scattered; they're all over the place, happily jumping on you or just hanging out with their mouths open, tongues lolling. A wolf's energy is much more focused. There is an incredible, peaceful intensity to it, a calm strength just below the surface that really is spiritual. It's been said that a wolf's eyes can see into your soul. I can understand why. For all of the day-to-day challenges, just spending time in the enclosure with them always gave me a great sense of peace. It was like meditation… with tummy rubs.

Speaking of that laser focus, an odd phenomenon took place early on when the wolves first came to live with us. In the mornings I'd be sleeping when suddenly, I would awaken feeling as though someone was watching me. After this had happened a few mornings in a row, I woke up and looked out the window that faced the wolf pen. There, down in the enclosure, three sets of slanted eyes peered up at me. The wolves were lined up, staring intently at the bedroom window. I guess we had a pretty strong energetic connection, because whatever they were doing was effective! This happened morning after morning until I finally decided to ignore the behavior, and thereby not reward the wolves for their efforts. It worked.

People often ask how long wolves live in captivity. Ours lived to be thirteen. The boys were with us for ten years, and Sequoia, who was three years older, was with us for seven. Sequoia passed first, and the boys passed two years later, six months apart. In fact, Phantom passed only three short weeks after Mojo did. It took me a very long time to stop automatically looking over at their enclosure every time I drove up the hill to our house. I still miss their howls. One day, when I too cross over the Rainbow Bridge, I hope to hear that beautiful welcoming chorus once again, along with the joyous greetings of all the dogs and wolves I have ever known and loved.

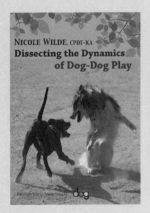

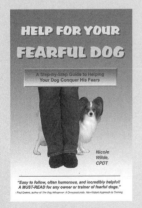